DALI'S

ANIMAL CRACKERS

by

A. Reynolds Morse

SALVADOR DALI MUSEUM, INC.
1000 THIRD STREET SOUTH
ST. PETERSBURG, FLORIDA 33701

Dali's Animal Crackers

by A. Reynolds Morse
assisted by Joan R. Kropf

Dali's Animal Crackers
is privately published by the
Salvador Dali Museum, Inc.
a non-profit corporation.

Cover: *The Elephants* by Salvador Dali, 1961; Detail.
©1993 Indianapolis Museum of Art.
Gift of Mr. and Mrs. Lorenzo Alvary.

Copies of *Dali's Animal Crackers*
are available only from:

Salvador Dali Museum
1000 Third Street South
St. Petersburg, Florida 33701
Telephone: (813) 823-3767

© 1993 SALVADOR DALI MUSEUM, INC.

The publication of *Dali's Animal Crackers*
was made possible through the generosity
of the Board of Trustees of the
Salvador Dali Museum, Inc.

INDEX

Dali: "myself is no likee-ee les animals.
              Is no one An-i-mal painter."

Morse: "On the contrary, Dali,
              you painted animals all the time."

Dali: "Is necessary you read (write) one book pour
              proof dees. Is absolutely necessary proof que Dali
              is no lof (love) les animaux."

(Conversation en route to Del Monte, California, Thursday, March 21, 1963.)

INTRODUCTION

I

This is the first attempt to take any kind of a look behind Dali's highly visible genius and to see firsthand just what an amusing and intensely vibrant human being the Catalan painter actually was. It is also the first vignette ever attempted by any biographer to reveal a totally impolitic and unknown side of his rutilant effervescence.

So far, most of our glimpses of Dali have come from people trying to size up his multifaceted personality without ever having had any actual pre-experiences with their subject. Thus, some extracts from my journal will reflect on-the-spot observations of the artist himself vis-a-vis various animals.

In sharp contrast to the tense, iconoclastic and agitated young Catalan who wrote *La Femme Visible* of 1930 and *The Conquest of the Irrational* in 1934, there clearly exists yet another Dali. This happily impish side of the surrealist philosopher is almost totally unknown to those still trying to comprehend the artist's complex personalized surrealism and the involved thrust of his serious art. Certainly not one biographer so far has even mentioned Dali's fabulous bestiary.

Thus to offset the rigid disciplinary exercises of analyzing the two aforementioned challenging books, it is well to temper them with a less academic and uncomplicated subject such as Dali's animals. This will also help liven up the somewhat desiccated figure which today's academia still attempts to make of Salvador Dali as it tries (always unsuccessfully) to categorize his art and his role on the 20th Century scene. Worse still, Dali is being emasculated and bowdlerized at every turn, so that both his humor and wisdom are gradually being stripped away in the repeated attempts to normalize every aspect of genius and reduce it to a conventional norm. Even the extraneous word "fock" (pronounced fog) had to be deleted from a 1970's tape when Dali was declaiming about his giraffe. The pity is the real Dali is being pruned down to the level of a Miro, a Magritte or a Tanguy and his other, far less extraordinary, contemporaries whose personalities never seemed to get in the way of their creative art.

Before recounting this special facet of the Dali adventure, it should be recorded that the subject of animals exists fragmentally in a Dali Journal which I belatedly began in 1956. There "animals" become sort of an aside or interjection into the ongoing Dalinian history which was being recorded as it occurred. Today, this Dali Journal has turned me into a kind of mini-Boswell to Dali's Johnson as my mother once prophesied many years ago.

It is definitely not my intention here, however, to subsume in any way the Dalinian interludes and observations made of Dali over the past forty-eight years. These are still ongoing and are in a totally different historical category than Dali's bestiary which over the years grew into a distinct entity all its own.

Another such totally separate aspect of Dali exists in the notes and charts of the painter's business organization and the structure of his royal court as courtiers, publishers and exploiters of his genius came and went. Indeed, by the mid 1970's "Dali unincorporated" was grossing some eleven to twelve million dollars (all cash, of course) along with no questions of rights or royalities ever being raised. Thus, the story of Dali's business affairs deserves its own analytical study revealing still another facet of Dali's enormous vitality and varied talents.

II

The genesis of Dali's animals is really rooted in a trip to Europe which we took in early May 1974, when we accompanied Gala and Dali on the last voyage of S. S. France to Cannes and then going on to Port Lligat by car.

We went to New York a few days early at Dali's request. He had just decided to get rid of his hot tempered aide de camp "Captain" Peter Moore an astute Irish adventurer. Moore had fortuitously appeared in the early 1960's, just at the juncture where Dali's wife Gala had decided she was tired of being the artist's business manager, baggage handler, keeper of the ocelot, housekeeper and so on. By 1974 the couple had also begun to wise up to the fact that Moore had gone from being a penniless but increasingly bold opportunist, to becoming a millionaire on his take from Dali's lucrative art business. It was a tense moment in Dalinian history, especially after the couple found Moore was working both sides of the street, as they say, and decided that the man had to go.

At this time, Dali was just closing a show at the Knoedler Gallery, and I had accompanied him to the gallery for some last minute negotiations. Here my journal continues:

"En route back to the hotel, we had discussed two other subjects. One was Dali's animals. He was very excited about the octopus, the unicorn, the hippopotamus, the elephant, the swan, the sea urchin, etc. I told him that another vital project was a list of his portraits. He said, 'Is no so interesting, les portraits, parceque quand is pose, myself eez always forcéd make les concessions. Et is necessary change le nose ou le eye-ee pour please le clee-ant. Is necessary, mais in any way is alzo changing le character of le verk, et is no reveal que (what) Dali is see exactly. Is no le same que les animaux. Is too co-mer-ci-all les portraits et now myself is no make any more.' "

Assemblage of the Dali menage for the annual departure to Catalonia proved to be an enormous job. The artist also had taken a couple of rooms on the top floor of the St. Regis where he had been doing lifesize figure paintings using nude models. These he first covered with red fingerprint dust after which he arranged the girls so as to leave the imprint of their bodies on huge sheets of paper. Then he would later fill in such details as he wanted, and doing it so expertly that one could not tell the imprint from the sections he skillfully drew in. Needless to say, the studio rooms were total chaos as the painter packed up a few brushes and a bottle of the dust, etc., from the debris of the body print sessions, which I called lazy man's art. He defended his experiments by saying nobody else had ever thought of such an idea, conveniently overlooking Yves Klein's experiments of 1962.

During the preparations for the sea voyage, Dali's aide "Captain" Moore was very scarce since he was well on his way to being permanently separated from the menage as Dali's aide de camp and keeper of the ocelots. The Dalinian logistics were massive, as I often had occasion to verify the hard way. This time it included Gala's giving me a handful of bills and having me go pay their tabs at various restaurants including Laurent amounting to well over ten thousand dollars. When I returned with the receipts and the remainder of the cash, I recall the time we had opening and closing one of her bulging suitcases so she could stuff the balance of the money in among her clothing.

In addition to their usual luggage, there was also a large case of priceless drawings. These had been loaned to our Cleveland Dali Museum by the artist, and I was elected to hand carry it during the trip back to Port Lligat.

Eleanor was pressed into the dubious role of keeper of the rabbit. This was a huge, four foot high, blue Bugs Bunny that Dali had received as a gift and which he loved extravagantly, precisely because it was so "oogly." Eleanor,

the rabbit and Dali went in one cab while Gala and I took another to the pier for the noon departure. There Gala spent an hour scanning the pier for her boyfriend Jeff Fenholt, the star of "Jesus Christ Superstar," who never showed to say goodbye.

When we finally got the couple settled in their stateroom on the ship, the artist explained to the noisy horde of excited reporters that he was taking the Bugs Bunny back to Catalonia because he wanted to transform it into a surrealist object by covering it with mayonnaise. Meanwhile, the photographers were having a heyday with Dali, the rabbit and Eleanor, all three sitting on the sofa.

In order to understand the penance involved in having Eleanor carry the big "oogly" Bugs Bunny which was almost as tall as she was, it is necessary to go back a decade to Wednesday, March 20, 1963, and its inception in Chicago of all places.

The Bugs Bunny fetish had first surfaced when we were between trains with the Dalis' in the windy city en route to California. It was Easter time and store windows everywhere were full of rabbits.

The purpose of the trip was for Dali to do a portrait of a Mrs. Briggs whom he had painted originally in the early 1940's when the Dalis' were staying at Del Monte Lodge in Pebble Beach. It was only after many frenetic conferences that it was eventually concluded to make the journey. The sitter by now had four children whom she wanted to include in her new portrait. So Gala had decided quite logically that it was far more feasible to transport one artist to Carmel than to bring four children to New York.

Eleanor Morse and the "oogly Boogs Bunny"

We had boarded the artist's train when it stopped in Cleveland, and thus soon found ourselves having lunch in Dali's favorite Chicago restaurant the Pump Room in the Ambassador Hotel. After lunch the master insisted we visit some antique shops, so we taxied to lower Michigan Avenue and began the rounds.

On an upper floor we entered a large shop where the fat female proprietor sat ensconced in her easy chair, reading a newspaper and paying no attention to us at all.

I was across the rather large room from Dali when he began to become very agitated. He silently tried to impart a sense of urgency to me visually, with violent amusing gestures, signals and grimaces. I did not comprehend his meaning and blithely went on with my own search for obelisks. Finally, he gave up and came over to me. In a whisper he said, "Morse you is no see nossing?"

I replied, "What did you mean, Dali? What was the excitement all about?" He explained, "You is no look le animal? Is seeng one beaver!" "Beaver?" I replied. "Yes," he said. "Myself is make-ee le signal for you to come look le beaver."

It then evolved that the proprietor had been sitting in her chair, reading a full-spread newspaper which she was holding up in front of her. She was sort of leaning back with her feet up on a recliner and one could look right up and see "one black an-i-mal!" Dali said.

As we left the store, Dali gleefully recounted the beaver story to Gala and Eleanor, taking great pains to illustrate all his unsuccessful graphic attempts to attract me over to his viewing position from which he had a protracted view of the woman's pudenda. Several times later he teased me about missing his sighting of "one black an-i-mal!"

It was this trip to Carmel in the 1960's that "Boogs Boonny" along with "Rising Cemented Toast" became key words in our private vocabulary. These codes the master would inject into his conversation with his various guests, clients and hangers on, much to their mystification. To us it was a signal that he was getting bored with the court riff-raff and "decorative people" and that we should move to break up the assemblage so the four of us could retire to a quiet corner at the King Cole Bar in the St. Regis Hotel for a "night cap" and some strategic conversation. The former, in his case, was always "acidophilus milk." ("It is create le most dee-vine excrement, et ess sleep very well.").

Indeed, "Rising Cemented Toast," already long a private Dalinian code word had also originated in Chicago. It was on February 6, 1952, when we were with the Dalis in Chicago en route to Iowa State Teacher's College in Cedar Falls, Iowa. There Dali was to give a spectacular lecture during which he predicted that the molecule of life would have a spiral form when it was ultimately discovered. We were having tea in the Bali (Dali) Room at the Blackstone Hotel when Dali tried to order raisin cinnamon toast. This in Dalinese came out "Rising Cemented Toast," to the total confusion of the waiter. We tried to straighten the matter out: Gala in Russian, Eleanor in French, Spanish, Italian, and Dali in Catalan and myself in German, after which it evolved the waiter spoke mainly Greek! And so originated our first private code word that was to relieve many a tedious situation over the ensuing years. Now to continue with the genesis of the "oogly Boogs Bunny," a decade later.

After our shopping tour, we hailed a taxi to take us to the station. En route, Dali suddenly spotted a "Boogs Boonny" in a store window. It was extremely ugly. We all got a glimpse of it in the crepuscule, and Gala refused to obey Dali's command to "Stop le car! Myself is catch le Bugs Bunny." The ladies convinced him we simply did not have time left to stop, and so we drove on over his rather agitated protestations that he wanted the rabbit precisely because it was so "oogly"!

The incident became a frequent subject of debate between us, for Dali never forgave or forgot any such brazen intrusion into his kingship such as the disobeying of an order or a royal command.

Thus over some ten years later, after some passing admirer caved in and gave him a HUGE ugly Bugs Bunny, he finally took his revenge on us for not letting him buy the much smaller version years ago in Chicago! The upshot was that for the next fortnight it was Eleanor who was delegated to carry the monstrous rabbit to the boat, through Cannes and on to Port Lligat. And the mayonnaise? It never materialized, and while we never learned the ultimate fate of his giant ugly rabbit, the secret key words remained in effect until his final decline began in 1980. "Is look le Boogs Bunny" thus mysteriously appearing in a conversation incongruously, would thus let us know when he had had enough of the interview or whatever, and that it was time we moved on.

III

On this voyage to Cannes in 1974, we were to see very little indeed of the Moore fellow and his wife who kept the ocelots in their cabin. The aide was bitterly jealous of us, even though it was at the end of his tenure. And particularly he resented our usurping his role in the Dali household, even momentarily, innocently and quite by chance. He was also aware, of course, that we had heard the Dalis' side of his various depredations, and that as old friends, we were fully appraised of the reasons for the arrival of Enrique Sabater as his replacement. Moore, far more than Sabater, bitterly resented our familial relationship with the couple and the fact that we had already known Dali for more than a decade before he first appeared on the scene. Indeed, his comments about me in a projected book were highly uncomplimentary to say the least.

Moore even carried his vendetta against me to saying in a *Life* Magazine article that Eleanor and I had met Dali in the men's room at the St. Regis Hotel in 1943. Actually, we had a drink with him at his invitation in the King Cole Bar, while nobody seems to have questioned how Eleanor would have gotten into the men's room to meet Dali there!

In fact, I think we only saw Moore once and for the last time on the trip to France when we all had dinner with the Dalis on the ship. Dali was totally enthralled at the bitter hostility generated by our being on board and by Moore's visibly glowing jealousy over our presence which he took no pains to hide. King Dali ruled us all with a strong hand, playing us against each other as suited his immediate aims.

In our case, we were clients and old friends, while Moore was in the unenviable position of a discarded servant whose usefulness to the court of Dali was expiring. The artist relished the adversarial positions, and savored the discomfitures involved with all the glee of a whimsical monarch.

The fact remains that Moore and Sabater both became millionaires in turn on the money they made waiting on the artist and his wife, garnishing well-earned but lucrative commissions in the process and accumulating wealth far beyond their fondest expectations.

It was therefore, from this voyage to Cadaques with Gala and Dali in the spring of 1974 that there continued to evolve the concept of a Dalinian bestiary. The idea was to recount the painter's fables, allegories, his fanciful and often moralistic stories about the array of creatures he had known over his lifetime, and enigmatically depicted in so many of his paintings, while meantime leaving his friends and critics baffled over his "Surrealist" symbolism and references to his private bestiary.

In the spring of 1974, the painter was in a mellow mood and at the very peak of his fame. And he was especially excited over the idea of creating a new book to relieve the tedium of the voyage.

IV

At this point it is relevant to mention my journal of April 24, 1974, and the recorded beginning of the evolution of the Dalinian bestiary. Parenthetically, it might be observed that I did attempt to use a tape recorder for the first and only time in all our Dalinian sessions over the years. The noise in the Dürer bar made conversation undecipherable, however, and I never before or since attempted to tape Dali's words. Thus in the end, it is mainly in my journal which was written each evening after our interviews, that one can capture the flavor of the genesis of the Dalinian animal adventure as it actually began, and as I was able to add to it over the years during our subsequent visits and travels with the Dalis.

Gala took far less pleasure in these narratives than the artist and ourselves. Often she would absent herself entirely from our animalistic explorations with the painter and the occasionally raunchy episodes involved.

Here then follows an extract from the Dali Journal: (Manuscript Vol. 27. typed Volume 9, November 13, 1972 through May 11, 1974) It is the entry for April 24, 1974, aboard S. S. France en route to Cannes.

At ten of eight we went up to the bar. Dali was invisible, so I asked the headwaiter if the master was there He said, "Yes, in the rear corner." And there, hidden away, were Gala and Dali. "Why is you no come sooner?" Dali asked almost plaintively. "What were you doing all afternoon?" "Fucking," I replied, and he glanced quizzically at me before he started to talk. The master was wound up for bear and zeroed in on me at once. Our total conversation for forty minutes centered around two main ideas—for Dali shakes a bone thoroughly: the former Hartford Museum, which he felt was a natural ready-made to house our Dali Collection and a new book about Dali's animals. He began with the second and more feasible and more interesting topic.

Dali said his animals would be a new project. He told me to get out my pencil and paper. I said I had none, and that I was here to relax, not to work. "Never mind," he said, "we will talk. In any way, le mouth, le mandibles is le source of everything! Now is feerst le teetle (title). Dali's—avec un s'—Dali's Animal Crackers! is le name. Is very good, no?" I said (when I could get a word in), "Was he aware we would be identifying with the Marx Brothers' movie of the same title?" "Of course," he retorted. "Is le best way." He tapped his head with his forefinger, and then using his cane to punctuate his words, he went on to indicate that he had been ratiocinating and was well ahead of us. "Quand dees words is already exist in le mind of les peoples, is no necessary so much promotion. Is already familiar. Is necessary only write (read) le book, et les peoples is buy at once. Is one success. Is ready made."

He said that Halsman's wet cats would be ideal for the cover. We would have to get Halsman's permission, of course, but that would be very easy "parceque Halsman is one good friend."

"Feerst is le vorm. Le vorm in le cherry." Eleanor then said, "the bat." He said, "Yes, quand y yam very jung is foods (ate) one bat. Everysing important is start in le mouth. Et then is le carp." "Oh, no, Dali," I shot back.

"The carp is a very dirty fish, and you never had anything to do with a carp." "On le contrary," he said, "is one new injection, le carp. Is start right now. Le history is dees. Quand le carp is becoming very old, les scales is grow very large. Si you is remove les scales et dry. Suedently is becoming one musical instrument. You is place two dry scales of le carp in le mouth—everysing is commence in le bouche, le...le..." "Mandible," said Eleanor. "Si," he went on, "mandible, le mout, si you is putsch le dry scale in le mouth et blow, le air is become music exactly like le clarinet, more beautiful que Benny Goodman. Is use in Roumania. Les carps in le Danube is become very old, et is become le music. Et is no arrive le staircase of Damien, so is one continuity avec le carp! Now is feeneesh. Is already read (write) one book in three menoots (minutes)."

Irreverently I responded. "Baloney. You do this all the time Dali. You say, 'feeneesh in three minutes,' and then you let some other poor bastard do all the real work. But still it is a great idea, even the carp, and we should do it." "Et no forget in *Journal d'un Genie* myself is tell le story quand y yam paint your picture *Nature Morte Evangelique.*" "*Eucharistic Still Life,*" I interjected, but he persisted "Evangelique. Myself is very preoccupied avec le feesh que is fly-ee, how you say dees?" "Flying fish," I put in. "Exactly. In le *Journal* myself is tell about le picture. Is very preoccupied about Matila Ghyka et les proportions." "In the square root of five divisions," I said. "Exactly," he went on. "Is completely mathematical, dees picture, mais is included le flying fish. Is one udder for le book." (*Diary of a Genius,* Doubleday, 1956. Entry of July 1, 1952.)

For some fifteen years these various animal notes have awaited expanding beyond the limits of the Dali Journal and as recorded in Manuscript Volume 9, covering the period November 13, 1972 through May 11, 1974. Now that the painter is dead and ourselves getting along in years, it becomes more important than ever to record these often hilarious interpretations of Dali's own animal kingdom. They show an amusingly human side of an artist who really did not care for animals at all! (Some proof of this fact is found under C for CATS beyond.)

Since there is no real hegemony in Dali's private zoo, there is no way to account for it other than to treat it alphabetically.

"Now is necessary you is make-ee les notes of les animals of Dali. Et is possible illustrate et create le book *Animal Crackers.* You verk on dees." So eighteen years later I am at last obeying the King's command!

V

THE SECRET LIFE OF SALVADOR DALI

Vision Press, London, 1942 (Editions 1961-1976, etc.)

No study of insects and animals in Dali's life is complete without a thorough reading of his early autobiography first published in 1942. When I finally made the index appearing in later editions of this introspective and self-analytical book, it never occurred to me that I should have been more thorough and included all his fabulous references to living creatures which impacted his life and which he recorded in his early (1942) recollections. Anyone interested in assessing this aspect of

Dali and the influence of creatures in his life should, therefore, by all means read *The Secret Life of Salvador Dali:* No other artist of the 20th Century has so completely disclosed his own evolution and the sources of his private cosmogony.

The most amazing feature of Dali's *Secret Life,* however, is how many people try to assess the artist's revelations after having read the book, then fail entirely to realize just how well the painter himself has explained the sources of so many of his seeming quirks and eccentricities.

The superb drawings with which he illustrated his *Secret Life* in themselves comprise a monument to Dali's draftsmanship which have been exhibited at the Pompidou in 1980 and in the Dali Museum, November 1982 to June 1983, as well as in Zurich in 1989, etc.

The painter's subsequent book *Diary of a Genius* (Doubleday 1965 and reissued in 1986 by Prentice Hall Press) also contains many examples of the Dalinian bestiary. It sporadically covers the years 1952-1963, but its index is not aimed either at animals or other such specific aspects of his life, although there are many references to fish and swans, etc., reflecting his closeness to the sea and the picturesque countryside where he always lived most of the year. There he was far closer to nature than any of his contemporaries as his later works continue to demonstrate.

His *Fifty Secrets of Magic Craftsmanship* published in 1947 gives still further proof of Dali's preoccupation with various animals, but it does not, alas, really live up to the book's title for the artist's real secrets are purposefully lost in his typically amusing, but frustrating, obfuscations.

In a small book titled *Dictionario Privado de Salvador Dali* (Recopilado y ordenado por mario Merlino) Altalena Editiones S.A., Madrid 1980, Dali lists several of his favorite animals including a "Bestiario," along with Grillos, Homigas, Moscas and Rinoceronte, etc. These are amusing and incontrovertibly proof that Dali has always been preoccupied with various animals, but in his own unique way. Thus, where applicable, the painter's own words are quoted as found in Dali's *Private Dictionary*.

Certainly anyone assessing Dali's bestiary also has to include his numerous illustrations for various books over the years, for they are replete with references to many of the creatures listed in this index.

To me, as a student of Dali and his thought processes, he seems unique among modern artists for his treatment of living things from anchovies to worms, abetted of course by one of the most lively and all encompassing imaginations the world of modern art has ever seen.

By looking precisely at the details of his handling of animals, Dali emerges as he really was, a whimsical amusing man who made a career of always serving up a most unexpected fare, and doing so with a flair for abandon and deftness of pen and thought which shows why so many of his (jealous) detractors are relentlessly forced into admitting what we heard over the years more frequently than any other characterization of Dali: "I admire Dali's draftsmanship, but...."

By zeroing in on Dali's Animals, however, one can avoid all the other challenges his works contain and which even today frustrate many of his admirers looking for esoteric meanings, symbols and details which make his art so much more challenging and fascinating than most of his more repetitive contemporaries.

diccionario
privado de

SALVADOR
DALI

recopilado y ordenado
por Mario Merlino

altalena

This is also a unique book because I know of no other artist who can merit an entire volume devoted to just one small facet of his art where the entire emphasis is on details such as those Dali himself outlined in 1974. As Dali was different from the 20th Century mainstream of art, so is *Dali's Animal Crackers* different from other art books trying to flesh out proponents–painters–of other eras who recreated their own weird and wonderful imaginary worlds, all of which Dali knew well, but which he studiously avoided replicating, especially Bosch and Breugel.

"Animal Cracker Topics and Notes" are found in holograph manuscript, Volume 17, 1974 of my unpublished journal. They form the basis for this study. The subjects are here re-arranged in alphabetical order, and derive from countless conversations with Dali which began in 1943 and ended in 1980.

Readers of *Animal Crackers* will note that many headings are followed by a brief text, sometime in quotes. The initial introductions to each animal are thus taken directly from my notes, and our extended conversations with Dali, as we enlarged on the idea of the present book on the S.S. France and elsewhere over the years. The transition sometimes may seem abrupt from Dali's own comments at the outset of the texts, to my own expansion of them that follows. I have tried to give some of the flavor of his unique English spoken with Spanish and French pronunciations. His English was as good as he wanted it to be. It became more French and Spanish accented in proportion as he sized up his interlocutor and his own boredom with the interview. In business negotiations he was sharp as a tack and there was no problem whatsoever with language so long as money was involved.

DALI'S ANIMAL CRACKERS

Telephone in a Dish with Three Grilled Sardines at the end of September — *1939* — 18 x 21⅝ inches.

ANCHOVIES
(AND SARDINES)

Now is remember que arrive les silver scales avec many reflections

SALVADOR DALI

April 27, 1974. In the bar of the S.S. France, about 12:45 p.m., we asked Dali about anchovies. At first he seemed a little blank. Then he began, "Oh, yes. Is OK. Now is remember que arrive les silver scales avec many reflections, *ebluissant,* and one enormous qvuantity of anchovies et sardines. Is see dees many times in le sea, et is very beautiful. Is le same que le light in le *Tuna Fishing.* Now is necessary catch one sack, very klar of polyester resin que is prevent le putrefacation, et is throw in me swvimming pool pur catch le light of le silver et white in les scales of l'anchovey."

"Now is necessary you is make-ee les notes of les animals of Dali. Et is possible illustrate et create le book *Animal Crackers.* You verk on dees."

When we were staying as the only guests in the primitive Hotel Port Lligat in 1954 and before the Dali's arrived from Rome, Rafael Pell, the proprietor would start our bleak dinner with one anchovy. One evening Eleanor wanted another, and I went out into the kitchen with our plates for a refill. Sr. Pell reached under the rather dirty sink and pulled out a revolting, smelly, uncovered large mouthed bottle, and with two dirty fingers pulled out two more anchovies from the vile, brown, salty liquid.

Later I told the master about it when we were having dinner with the Dalis in their house and how bad the bottle smelled. He admitted the hotel was terrible, but assured us the anchovies were not poisonous and that was the way they were commonly stored: open and under the kitchen sink!

The Costa Brava between the Bay of Rosas and the Gulf of Lyons is extremely rugged. The shoreline between Llansa, the last town in Spain and Rosas to the South, is rocky, forbidding and inaccessible. Cape Creus, the eastern most point of Spain, and Cape Norfeo south and west of Cadaques, both plunge precipitously into the sea. These waters make for superb fishing, and the run of fish whether it be tuna or anchovies provided exciting times, more so in the past than today.

When in residence in Port Lligat, Dali subsisted mainly on fish with an occasional pigeon from his tower-like dove cot, a major and busy feature of his hillside garden. Fried anchovies (sardines) were one of his favorite foods, though I do not specifically recall his often eating the salt preserved fish we identify as anchovy. His favorite starter was really little neck clams.

Untitled oil — 28 X 41 inches

DALI'S
ANIMAL CRACKERS

On April 25, 1974 aboard the S.S. France, Salvador Dali settled down in the first class bar. He sat in a large leather chair, placed his crossed hands on his silver-headed cane and said, "Now, les ani-mals." I began by citing some examples of animals in his paintings. These he rejected at once, saying, "No. Only les anee-mals que is show que y yam one complete jay-ni-us. Le tur-tel is one le most important. Feerst le turtle." (See under "T" beyond.)

ANIMALS

Animals (Dali: Ah-nee-mals)

The work pictured here is untitled. It is an oil (28 x 41 inches). It was commissioned by a friend of Dali who "liked animals." The artist asked him, "What kind?" "Any kind" his client replied. Dali said that he was not really very enthusiastic about "animals," but the man persisted, and this untitled work was the result.

On April 18, 1972, it was offered to me for $65,000 by Barry Hill Galleries in New York. It is an amusing and atypical canvas, but withal not overly Dalinian in mood.

Many believed this work was a fake until I was able to show a photograph of it to Dali who told me he had only done it to accommodate a client, and not because he was inspired by animals per se. It has been reproduced in a full sized format and was not a best seller as it was not a "typical" or well advertised Dali work. Today it remains a whimsical canvas with the "Animals" relegated to a minor role, and redeemed from triteness by Dali's superb draftsmanship.

ANTEATER

*the animal was really quite docile
and behaved pretty well on Fifth Avenue.*
DALI

Rather early on we recall that Dali got the idea of appearing with an anteater on a leash. There was a considerable to do about the stunt, with Gala putting up many objections. The Master tried to enlist me in the project, but I had the courage to stay out of the negotiations with the people and the three hundred ants involved, much to his chagrin.

He did pull the stunt off, however, and was dutifully photographed by the press with the anteater on a leash walking the streets of New York. It seemed quite obvious, of course, after the ants got loose in Brentano's bookstore window that if Dali's ant obsession got any worse it might indeed be good to have an anteater handy. I remember Dali saying that the animal was really quite docile and behaved pretty well on Fifth Avenue.

André Breton
The Anteater

ANTS

Ants horrify me. In my work I paint what horrifies me,
the demoniacal, and what exalts me, angelic.

DALI

"**E**t no forget les ants dans le spectalcles que y yam create pour le Bestigui Ball. Is place les termeets inside les lenses por magnify. Is very terrifying." I reminded him of the ants in the Brentano bookstore window display. "Exactly," he commanded. "You take-ee note of dees!"

Salvador Dali's fascination with ants stems from his unique vision. His eyes could magnify even the most minute details. He loved to draw and paint the large ants such as abounded in the semi-arid countryside of Ampurdan. His eye glasses, double lensed with ants inside between the lenses always created a sensation. As a prop and attention getter, they enabled the artist to size up his audience and its reaction. His aim was to leave an indelible impression on the more receptive people who might become Dali converts.

Dali's double lensed glasses with ants inside

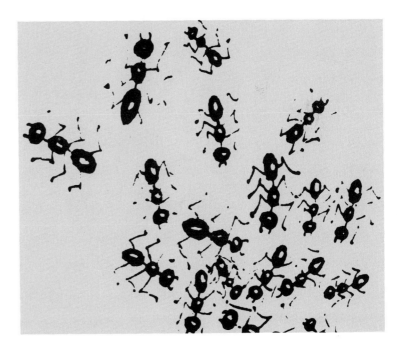

His ants are found in many drawings and today are an accepted symbol of his ability to depict the tiniest details. One of the most vivid examples of this fetish is found in his movie *Un Chien Andalou*. In the film a man's hand is caught in a door. As the fist opens, ants are seen in the protagonist's hands crawling in and out of a hole in the palm. It is one of those imaginative details that make *The Andalusian Dog* one of the cinema's most historic films.

How quickly and neatly he could draw an ant! One is seen in a drawing of an iceberg mostly underwater which he made (symbolizing his genius as being 75% obscured) while I was ill with tracheitis in Cannes on our way to Spain on May 1, 1974. It remains one of the three works Dali gave us over four decades.

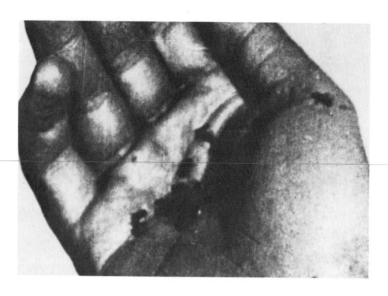

Ants in hand from the film *Un Chien Andalou*

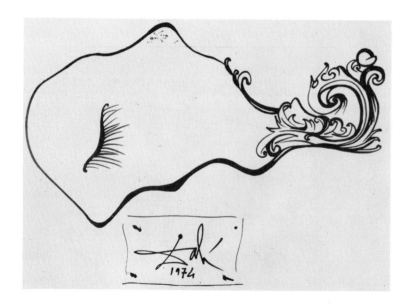

The Iceberg of Dali's Genius — *1974*

Study for a ceiling mural.

Bottom left: Early sketch of a man's hand with ants crawling out of a hole in it, used in the Dali—Bunuel film *The Andalusian Dog.*

Bottom right: Detail right center of sketch.

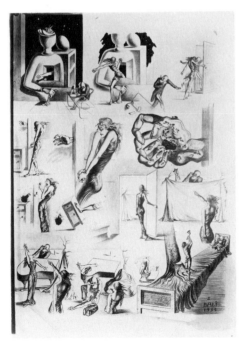

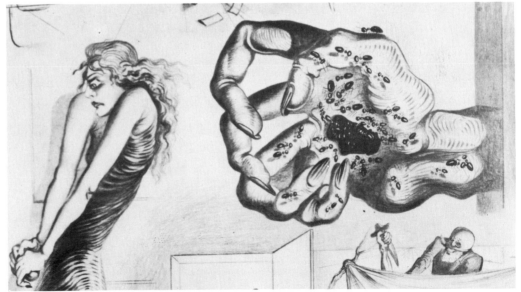

Another good example of Dali's ants is found in a design he did for Madame Schiaparelli in the mid 1930's. Dali made a great distinction between his easel paintings and his commissions and commercial designs. Today the art in commerce is often found for sale as Dali's art, when in reality, it was a commissioned work for use in commercial projects. The fact is, like *The Ants*, his commercial works are so well done that collectors will often buy them as his art. I often warned Dali of this, but he always downplayed the danger of his commissions becoming inter-mingled with his inspired work. In the case of *The Ants* watercolor, Dali did not want it in the Hartford Gallery show in 1965-6, but we showed it anyway.

As a youth in a rural town and in Cadaques, his super vision allowed him to capture ant details few artists could emulate. The shock value of his ants should not be overlooked for many people are truly terrified by them.

Dali Ants: *Design for Madame Schiaparelli.*

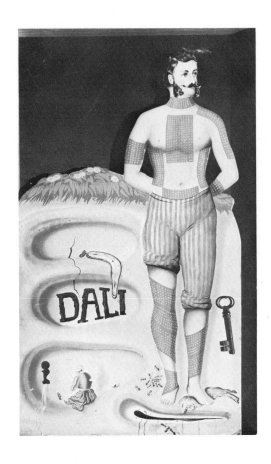

Surrealist Poster
1934 — 27 x 28 inches

To me Dali's ants are an unforgettable reminder that as man uses up the earth's irreplaceable resources, these creatures will become among the last terrestrial survivors. Thus his ants are among his most prophetic symbols.

Dali's command for real ants several times perplexed his early admirers. They were dismayed when the tiny city ants they somehow produced in New York were NOT the monster ants we associate with our western ones, or Dali's idea of ants as they are found in the barren region around Cadaques.

The main problem in realization of his fetish was further complicated by the difficulties involved in handling the ants in a hotel. Sensational though they were in Brentano's Fifth Avenue window, when they escaped even Dali had to admit that the stunt had its practical limitations.

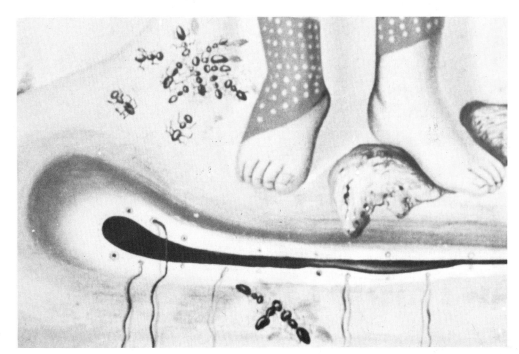

Detail: *Surrealist Poster lower right corner*

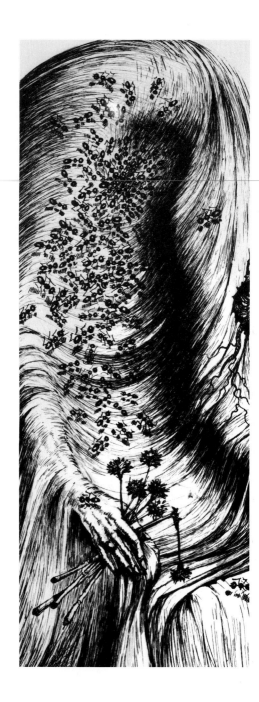

Top center:

Dali was a prolific book illustrator and ants found their way into many books—incongruously.

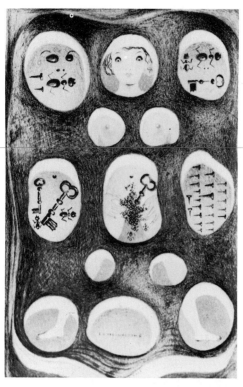

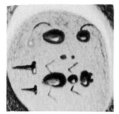

The idea of eyeglasses with live ants between a pair of lenses was a true paranoiac-critical concept that was really too much for the non-surrealist people of New York in the mid 20th Century. His image building, however, was a very definite and calculated factor and ants became a part of his show.

While his giant figures at the Bestigui Ball in Venice made the headlines, his ant glasses were totally overwhelmed and the media seems to have neglected them almost entirely.

The Bestigui Ball took place on September 3, 1951 at Labia Palace in Venice, and the Dalis appeared with six giant clowns seven meters high, and with themselves in costumes designed by Christian Dior, but the ants seem never to have made it into the record as far as can be determined.

Daddy Longlegs of the Evening...Hope!
1940 — 10 x 20 inches

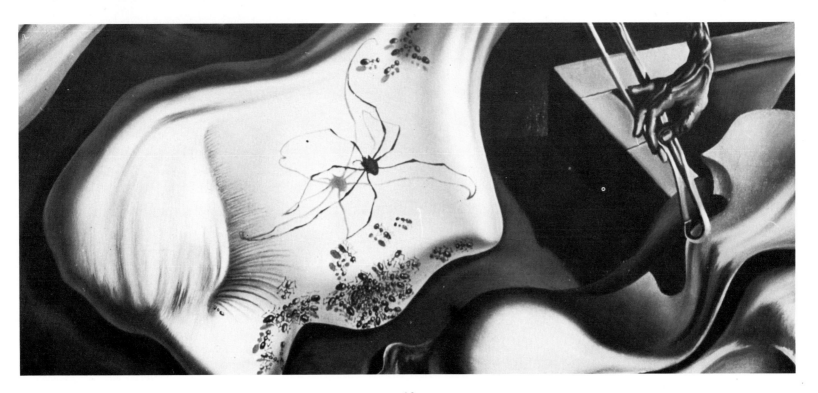

EXCERPT FROM DALI'S PRIVATE DICTIONARY

Ants horrify me. In my work I paint what horrifies me, the demoniacal, and what exalts me, angelic.

The other day I put a small bee under my shirt. Another time I put a box full of ants, illuminated by phosphorescent drops, over my eyes. Sometimes I do nothing.

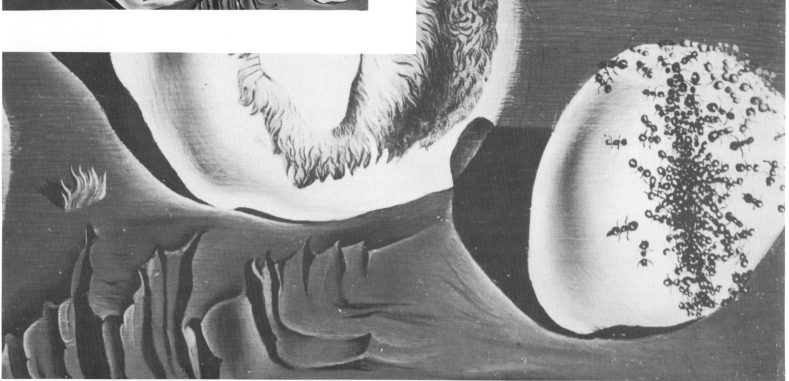

BATS

Even today the memory of this can give me the shivers, and often just seeing some black spots is enough to bring that bat's death back to me.   DALI

Bats are not often seen in Dali's bestiary. I recall Rosa Salleras telling us how as young friends in Cadaques they would go out in the crepuscule with long wands of cane. They would tie bits of cloth to one end of the cane on a string and would wave the poles around. The bats would try to follow and catch the bait. As they waved the wands in circles, the bats would become dizzy and confused and some would fall to the ground and be captured. Today, I am sure, Dali got his first look at a bat this way and never forgot the details. I asked Ms. Salleras how many bats they caught and she replied, "Very few!"

The bat adds an unforgettable touch to *The Enigma of Hitler* as it tugs at a soft object in the edge of the dish that contains Hitler's portrait. This symbolic canvas shocked the Surrealists, as they felt it was some sort of a pro-Hitler statement. The Dalis never sold the work. Indeed, I recall talking about it with Dali who did not want to be drawn out on it. It was surprizing, therefore, to find it among the various treasures they had stored away in Port Lligat against the reoccurrence of hard times, something they feared deeply. Their early years were not easy ones despite their bravura.

The bat on Shirley Temple's head where she is depicted as a "monster" or sphinx was a fun collage that was among the many works offered us which we did not purchase. It is now a museum piece.

"Shirley Temple, Le plus jeune monstre sacré du cinema de son temps," 1939

In *The Unspeakable Confessions of Salvador Dali* the artist rehashed some of his obsessions with animals already mentioned in his *Secret Life*. On page 14 of this book he refers to an incident with a bat — a rather grisly memory, but so vividly related that it holds a reader fascinated at its gruesome introspective frankness:

THE SECRET LIFE OF SALVADOR DALI, DIAL PRESS, 1943.

I am five years old. It is 1909. One of my cousins, who is twenty, has shot a bat in the eye with his carbine, and put it in a pail. I throw a tantrum, and demand that he give me the small animal, and then run to put it in one of my secret places, a warehouse that I often hide in. I watch the trembling, suffering little mammal, shrinking inside its prison. I speak to it, hold it, kiss its downy head. I begin to adore it. And the next day, first thing, I run to see it. I raise the pail, and find the animal already dying, lying on its back, with ants swarming over it; I can see its little panting tongue and the old man's teeth around its nose.

The Enigma of Hitler

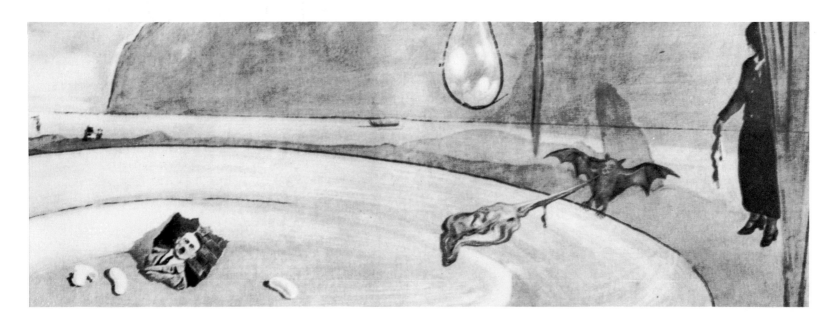

I regard it with infinite pity, then take it up and, instead of kissing it as I had first intended to do, suddenly in a kind of rage with one bite all but behead it. I am suddenly seized by the horror of what I have done, by the taste of blood I can feel in my mouth, and I frantically throw the little corpse into the washing vat at my feet alongside a large fig tree. I run away, tears streaming from my eyes. I turn back, however, but the bat has disappeared. Big black figs are floating on the surface of the water, like spots of mourning. Even today the memory of this can give me the shivers, and often just seeing some black spots is enough to bring that bat's death back to me.

Eleanor and Reynolds Morse in the Dali's front hall at Port Lligat

Dali's apartment at #10 Rue de la Université in Paris

Later its paws were seen to hold a silver tray which was always full of visitor's cards.

On May 22, 1992, Jordi Casals photographed Eleanor and myself in the front hall of Dali's house in Port Lligat showing the Edward James bear that once was in their apartment at #10 Rue de la Université in Paris before the house in Port Lligat was constructed.

BEAR

All visitors to Port Lligat were greeted by a large stuffed bear. This was an early gift from Edward James who was Dali's main mentor in the middle and late thirties. Mr. James ended up with a superb collection of early Dali works which were eventually sold at auction to sustain the James Foundation dedicated to the repair of old musical instruments (and, I believe also of farm implements).

When Eleanor and I first went to dinner at Dali's house in Port Lligat in 1954, the lights were not functioning. We came down from the hotel by flashlight. Katarina let us into the house and Eleanor's first sight of the bear by candle and flashlight scared her out of her wits. Many a visitor got a similar jolt, for nothing could be more incongruous in remote Port Lligat (reachable only on foot), than a huge bear.

BEEF

Boeuf Ecorcher

(The Side of Beef)

Dali's rendition of Scarlatti's opera *The Gladiator and the Roman Lady* with incongruous Dalinian backdrops was given in Venice on August 22-23, 1961.

In the staid historic theater, Dali's subsequent ballet with its huge ten to twelve foot soap bubbles made a hit.

One of his twists at the Fenice was to hang at stage center a bloody side of beef, flayed, the grisly inside facing the audience. When we tried to reason with him that it was in bad taste, he shot back that if Rembrandt can paint a *Boeuf Ecorcher* and have it hang in the Louvre, then Dali had every right to pay tribute to Rembrandt's work in the Teatro Fenice!

Even poor Lorenzo Alvary who was footing the bill for the spectacle (as well as singing in the Gladiator opera) tried to object, but Dali stood fast, and the fresh flenched side of beef was dutifully hung at the two performances in Venice and again at another one, I believe, in Amsterdam.

There was a modern painter, Chaim Soutine (1894-1943), at this time depicting fresh cut beef, and we feel Dali's *Boeuf Ecorcher* was really a slap at this artist who was also showing at the Carstairs Gallery. Dali was not to be outdone by anyone, anytime, and he certainly showed no admiration for Soutine's work which we felt was too heavy on dead chickens.

BEES

Dali had a figure cut into the schist rock of the hillside just to the right of the library door to the south patio, which the house sheltered from the tramontana. The natural sculpture was of a bare-breasted woman with the rock hollowed out back of it. The artist arranged the bust so that his hive of bees entered and left the little cave through the nipple of the figure. Not everybody appreciated his bee hive, but many of us found it both ingenious and amusing.

Also a mirror was set into a crack in the rocks adjacent to the house so as to reflect the dove cot back of the house where pigeons were raised for their table.

"Le poete"

On May 22, 1992, we visited Port Lligat with Lluis Peñuelas, Antonio Pitchot and Jordi Casals. The bee system was completely overgrown and I found the viewing mirrors in the crack in the natural schist wall all shattered and broken. So time moves on and with it Dali's magic also starts to fade. We found the lion in the garden and the giraffe both gone. The nostalgia of lonely Port Lligat brought back many moving memories of Dali and the happy hours we spent there when our friend was in residence and very involved with animalistic things from his swans to his little elephant and his attempt to get 500 elephant skulls for his garden. (Holograph Journal, Vol. 33, under May 22.)

The photograph taken by Jordi Casals shows me pointing out the spot on the cliff in Dali's garden in Port Lligat where the beehive breast once was found with Antonio Pitchot looking on. Today all traces of it are gone and it survives only in my memory of it.

BIRDS

The Catalan artist loved ortolans, (family: Brouant) a small sparrow-like ground nesting bird that is cooked crisp and eaten bones and all in France and Spain. Whether in Madrid, Barcelona or Paris, when ortolans were on the menu Dali would have them, while Gala partook only occasionally. The ortolan is considered a very effete sort of delicacy. We tried them both in Paris and Barcelona at Dali's insistence. If Gigi could cope with them — and Dali — so could we. My own verdict did not make the artist very happy; "an excellent source of calcium" but beyond that — were they really the delicacy Dali claimed? — or was it their growing scarcity both on the menu and in the field?

The artist also liked the torse(?), a game bird somewhat larger than an ortolan. And, of course, his pigeon house was always well inhabited, so pigeons were frequently on the painter's table in Port Lligat.

In the youthful gouache, *The Sick Child of 1914-15,* in the upper left a bird is seen in a cage. It has none of the

The Sick Child (1914-15)

23

The Ecumenical Council

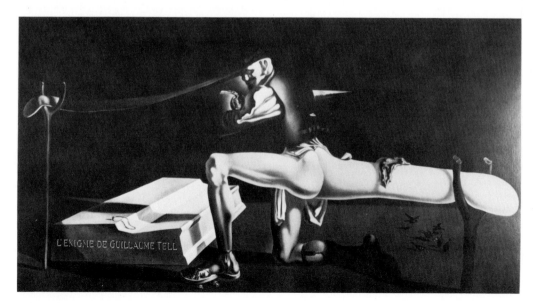

The Enigma of William Tell

fine detail seen in other later works such as *The Enigma of William Tell,* etc. Many of Dali's greatest surrealist works have several small birds hovering in them, including the huge *William Tell,* and other smaller canvases. Some of his avian subjects are somewhat distorted or generalized, especially in his earlier works such as *Le Vache Spectrale* and *The Ram.* Here the nod to Max Ernst is evident for Dali knew the works of his contemporaries well.

His *Madonna of the Birds* is by far the most successful of his several attempts to have flying birds form a visage in the sky. His study for such a bird-face figure was seen in a large format in a mural he did for Helena Rubenstein, where an artisan blew up his studies to mural size for the Rubenstein dining room. These were eventually peeled off the walls and sold as original Dali's when they were not, as I talked to the man who did the blowups myself.

The birds seen in *The First Days of Spring* refer to the use of parrots during the development of color film in the late 1920's. Birds were used (parrots especially) because of the way the light reflected from their surface. It gave an

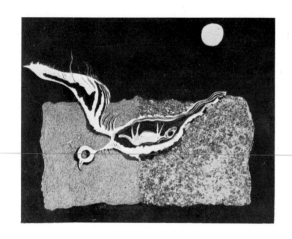
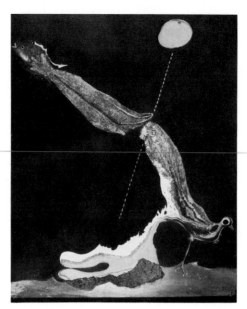

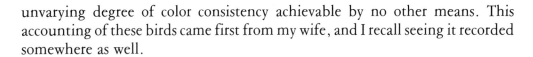

unvarying degree of color consistency achievable by no other means. This accounting of these birds came first from my wife, and I recall seeing it recorded somewhere as well.

The grasshopper and a fish's head, an early indication of the great masturbator's rock outline, along with a tiny goat show Dali's early use of animals in his works. Thus proving that his rural background left animalistic outlines which his paranoiac-critical creative method could retrieve and which were otherwise unaccountable. It was this factor that drove the art critics wild. Dali was not painting according to Hoyle so they simply belittled him. Grasshoppers, parrots, fish indeed! No other artist but Max Ernst and Marc Chagall would deign to put them on their canvases!

Dali's use of a bird done in dots to help create an imaginary *Portrait of My Dead Brother* in 1963 was interesting, but it somehow did not come off. A pseudo psychiatrist was working Dali over at the time, and the artist was trying to play up the dioscuri and to capitalize on the idea of the brother who died a year or so before he was born. His sincerity in this era seemed a bit too contrived and it did not really take in the entourage for a variety of reasons. It was a theme, however, that the artist took quite seriously.

Portrait of My Dead Brother

The major caveat here, is never to underestimate Dali's inherent talent. *The Dead Brother* portrait with its large bird formed in the upper dots remains an important experiment art wise and psychologically as well. The work is a rather large one and is difficult to view. And, of course, it is entirely an imaginary thing. It remains a fugitive piece, a bit poignant, but still something in which Dali's usual formula did not quite jell. He never explained the rational of the bird, so one can read virtually any meaning into his sudden belated revival of a brother he never knew. Today I feel the work is far better than I did when it was still imbued with "the shock of the new," and a possible addition to our collection.

Dali's birds—sparrows like ones in a feeding clutter are seen under the long hip in *The Enigma of William Tell* and in many other canvases, especially of the 1930's.

Several times in his early gravel collage of the late 1920's Dali nodded directly toward a form of decaying bird already made distinctive by Max Ernst. Some of his birds are quite fanciful, however, such as the one seen in *Cadaques Exquis,* a drawing.

During the very early 1940's Dali did several watercolors and even an oil or two where a flight of birds accidently became (or formed) a momentary face. The artist was obsessed both with the element of time and the coincidental appearance of an image made of extraneous random elements such as a group of birds caught in an instant of flight, when time actually stands still.

In those productive days it took some courage to make any sort of value judgement on a Dali work as it appeared. I was not much-impressed with Dali's birds until in April

The Madonna of the Birds

1943 at the Knoedler Gallery we saw *The Madonna of the Birds,* perhaps one of the top ten watercolors of his career.

It hung over our bed for more than two decades. It far outclassed all Dali's other attempts at catching the "bird faces" to the extent that we never bought another. I even passed up the version in Helena Rubenstein's dining room (made from a study by a craftsman into a mural) when the large canvas was taken off her wall and sold at auction as a Dali painting.

The tie in of *The Madonna of the Birds* to the immortal *Alba Madonna* of Raphael in the National Gallery of Art made the watercolor into a major paranoiac-critical work immortalizing birds in a way no other modern artist ever dared to conceive. And in 1943 not one reviewer spotted this work either as a great tribute to Raphael or something 100% more interesting than the abstract expressionists whose agonies they were all touting at the time.

The First Days of Spring — *1929*

The First Days of Spring — *detail*

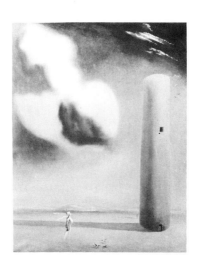

BULLS

"Ah Morse, you is speak le Spanish, mais myself eez know everysing. Les testi-cules is 'creador'." DALI

Bulls were always close to Dali's Spanish heart. He often went to bullfights in Figueres, Barcelona and Madrid. In one case in Figueres he had a helicopter come and haul the bull off to Heaven creating a spiritual or sacrificial scene in which he delighted, but which few of the spectators were able to interpret as the bull's soul supposedly soared off into infinity as it was bodily lifted up by mechanical means. Few indeed saw anything but another Dali stunt, not an exercise symbolizing the bull's spirit's departure from the ring.

The bull in *The Hallucinogenic Toreador* appears out of the cliffs of Cape Creus. It is taken from a particular Manolete kill, photographs of which are as common in Spanish barbershops as baseball stars' photos are in America.

We attended at least four bullfights with Dali. Gala liked the attention of the matadors who left their hats with her, while Dali loved the whispered adulation of the crowd around him. Since the bull's meat is sold at the arena, and is in much demand because of the adrenalin in the meat caused by the bull's anger, it seemed to us little different than the animal's treatment in an abattoir. Dali felt the bull always had a chance and took the whole ceremony with utmost seriousness.

Bottom left: Close up of a famous kill. Below is the large canvas *Hallucinogenic Toreador*. It can be seen in the Dali Museum of St. Petersburg where it (and its double image) is always on view.

I recall Dali telling about the disposal of the dead bull's meat at the arena. I asked him about the bull's testicles and were they the delicacy we had heard. I used the word "balls" and there ensued quite an attempt for me to come up with the Spanish word. After half a dozen attempts, Dali said, "Ah Morse , you is speak le Spanish, mais myself eez know everysing. Les testi-cules is 'creador'." (Which is in the dictionary is creator! Also criador-creator.)

33

BUMBLEBEE

(BOURDON)

BEE (ABEILLE)

Garcia Lorca often said Dali was like a bumblebee. The artist did have a habit of singing in a sort of buzzing sound when he was busy painting or preoccupied. When we were watching him work (which we did in total silence), he did indeed make this strange little noise with his mouth. Whenever I heard it, I always felt sad that I could not have met Garcia Lorca.

BUTTERFLIES

"No! No butt-err-fly-ees in Animal Crackers." DALI

When I suggested butterflies, Dali said, "No! No butt-err-fly-ees in Animal Crackers." (This was because he has so often used cutout butterflies in his hurry-up art, collages, etc.) Then he reconsidered. "Ah, yes!" and told how once he had caught a fish called a serra (?).Then he took a straw and inserted it in the anus of the fish and blew cigarette smoke into the fish, until after a while it began to come out of the mouth of the creature. Just at that precise moment, he said, there appeared three very beautiful butterflies of a sort he had never seen before. (Here I questioned him about the damn fish and finally got the spelling down in my notes.)

FROM SALVADOR DALI'S COLLECTION "MEMORIES OF SURREALISM"

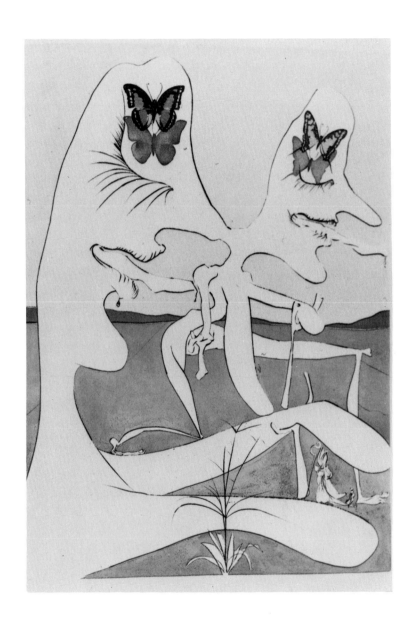

Especially during the 1950's Dali utilized butterflies in many ways. Several times we were sent to buy books containing butterfly illustrations for the artist to cut up and use as collages. It was often difficult to tell which butterfly was an illustration by the artist and which was a reproduction. From first hand observation, butterflies were not often seen in Alt Ampurdan. When butterflies appeared in his commercial designs they were often as not cutouts and for a decade he continued to utilize them decoratively, and with no special significance which we could determine. When I said his butterfly collages were a symptom of laziness he made no comment. A great many of his cutout butterflies went into ads such as those for Bryan Hosiery and other purely commercial commissions. And whenever a butterfly flew into his garden in Port Lligat, the artist would study it carefully.

Anyone who knew Dali at all well was surely treated to his famous lesson in (Dali's) English. The word butterfly came out as BOO-TER-FLY-EE and Dali loved to "perform" it as much as his courtiers liked to laugh at his little act of "hispanized" English.

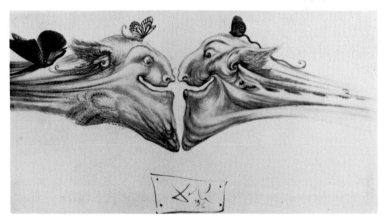

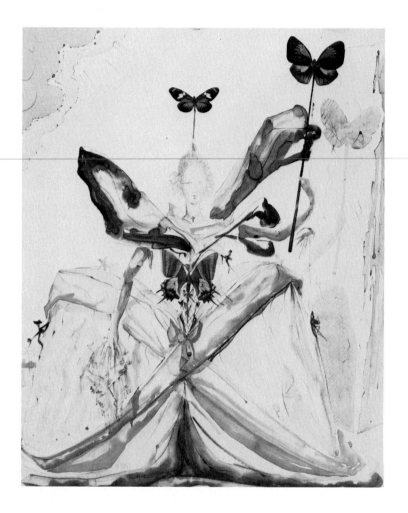

The artist was fascinated with the subject of mimesis —imitation of art and literature— and did a fascinating article on the subject in Fleur Cowles' spectacular 1953 Flair Annual (Salvador Dali's *Mimicry in Nature,* pages 200-206.) Here with deft cutouts, a butterfly becomes an owl, and beyond the two dots on the butterfly's wings then become the eyes of the girl in a painting as the cutout pages are turned.

Dali's article on insect mimesis is a classic tidbit. It is reproduced here because The Flair Annual for 1953 is today a rare book indeed and Dali's ideas on mimicry deserve a permanent place in his bestiary.

I vaguely recall one day during a walk in Port Lligat, that the artist spotted a leaf-butterfly on some plant. He challenged me to find it. When I was unable to, he took great delight in startling the butterfly into flight. He was especially proud over such displays of his knowledge of nature's ways for he was extraordinarily well versed on every aspect of nature in his native Ampurdan.

This is perhaps a good place to record a major Dalinian trait. Each season as he emerged from the comparative isolation of Port Lligat, the painter seized on some theme which he repeated with jolly emphasis as he moved on from Barcelona to Paris and New York.

Thus it was his habit to play up a single theme, such as his fanciful syllabification of "butterfly" with histrionic gestures and facial grimaces. His act had an indelible effect on his string of international admirers.

The artist's "themes" over the years included, for example, his featuring of ants and the anteater, soap bubbles, his arquebus and bulletism, his cruciform cubes used in Corpus Hypercubus, etc., etc.

Salvador Dali's

MIMICRY IN NATURE

Of ALL the wonders in Nature, the most surrealistic is beyond doubt the astonishing mimesis of insects. In the past year these outrageous insect mimics, these stars of vegetable impersonation, have repeatedly made headline appearances in books and journals, without anyone venturing to guess what this sudden popularity might mean, or whom it might affect.

The leaf-butterfly imitates a leaf in a manner worthy of the most refined and hypocritical of *trompe l'oeil* painters. Not only does it accomplish, through an extremely obscure and mysterious biological process, the reproduction on its wings of the finest veins of the plant, but it succeeds in imitating with a kind of malice and sublime coquetry the most subtle phenomena of mouldiness, and even the accidental holes caused by sunshine in drops of water. It can also imitate the exact shadings of burnt colors on leaves, through their gradual autumnal decay, then their utter dryness, and later the ammoniacal and half-decomposed color of wintertime.

Leaf-insects, stick-insects, thorn-insects, insects looking like a piece of rotten wood—why? Scientists first believed in a miraculous instinct of self-defense, self-preservation. Having become a leaf, the insect is invisible and passes unobserved among enemy insects dangerous to its kind. It is the theory of camouflage in modern warfare. But soon these scientists observed that, according to their experiments, the mimesis of the leaf-insect stemmed from a far less practical impulse than it had seemed at first. Indeed, they had not suspected this: disguised as a leaf, the insect may avoid a problematic fight with other insects, but falls prey to a far more implacable enemy. It now may be mercilessly devoured by birds taking it to be a leaf.

These convincing observations would then lead our scientists to a second theory: mimesis among insects obeys a kind of impetus, a universal will for self-annihilation, a mystical suicide from the particular to the general, a process of depersonification, of "total integration into the unity of the cosmos."

This theory, of great metaphysical beauty, is nevertheless contradicted once more by the existence — most incredible and marvelous of wonders — of the butterfly on page 200: pursued by birds, it turns on them suddenly to frighten them away with the appearance itself of a bird of prey!

Specialists on birds, leaf-insects and leaves will probably spend many more years trying to decide between the two opposite theories and not reach any conclusion. For, very likely, both theories are true, and thus bring to its crowning glory one of the deepest thoughts of Heraclitus, whose whole philosophy was built upon the harmony of opposites.

But while the scientists continue their polemics on the subject of leaf-insects and owlbutterflies, let the explosive imagination of Salvador Dali bring you the latest idea intercepted antenna-wise at the tip of his famous moustache. Yes! We are nearing the time of mimesis in feminine apparel, and the symptomatic presence of swarms of butterflies in the Paris collections was a feeble indication of the truth in my prophecy.

I have known Christian Dior ever since 1930, when we made the rounds of Paris in pursuit of a mutual floral passion, realized in the *objets d' Art Nouveau* of 1900 — which everyone then despised, and which the most fashionable ladies have since been forced to display upon their very exquisite bodies. Now I feel a period coming for leaf-women, stick-women, autumnal-wood-women. For owl-women who will also be butterflies, and butterflies that will also be rocks. Women who will disappear into the trees, who will disintegrate on a patch of moss, and whose silhouette will be of thorns tender as roses — roses transparent as a Lalique dragonfly wing. Mystical roses...

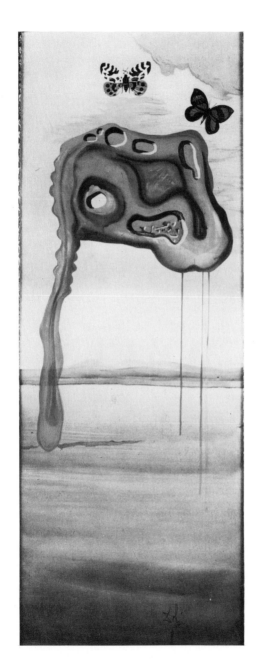

The logistics of his stuffed animals was a considerable problem in my opinion, but not in his. Both Arturo and Gala were very long suffering with these manifestations of Dali's living surrealism. In his private world they were essential props, from his elephant skull to the stuffed lion in the new garden off to one side of the dining alcove, with incongruity rampant - for opposing the lion was a female manikin dressed as a nun!

CAMELS

The tiny version of the camel in the nostalgic oil *Sun Table* stemmed from the appearance of a camel in the town of Beziers which adopted the animals as its official mascot. In 1974 as we drove by Beziers enroute to Cadaques, Dali said the town was presenting him with a stuffed camel for his garden and sure enough in due course it appeared. Beziers, he said, was where a man once lived who had an enormous penis. Each Sunday he would publicly display it for a few pesetas. People came from miles around for the sight. "Even from Figueres?" I asked. And he said, "Yes." It was one of the great attractions of the entire region. Dali's knowledge of his Alt Ampurdan countryside was profound and Beziers was proud to honor him.

Sun Table — *detail lower left*

Sun Table — *1936*

In the book *Captain Sir Richard Francis Burton* there is an interesting reference possibly relating to Dali's use of a camel in his oil painting called *Sun Table* of 1936. Certainly one reason Dali "interspersed a camel along with all the other elements" is that the artist was well aware of his Arabic blood. He loved the idea of mystic concepts. And Burton's biographer reminds us that it is "Death who, in Arabia, rides a camel and not a pale horse." We are still left, however, without knowing the identity of the strange man on Dali's camel. Is it the "Chemist of Ampurdan?" We shall perhaps never know!

It is too obvious to mention that of course the model for Dali's camel was that seen on the world renowned cigarette package. So far as I know neither Gala nor Dali ever smoked, and in the main visitors in his house had the courtesy not to do so. Even at his fabulous dinner parties, his beatnicks smoked very little if any in his presence.

CAPTAIN SIR RICHARD FRANCIS BURTON

Throughout, Sufi mystical concepts appear — wine as a symbol of mystical intoxication, the Potter and his pot, and "Death who in Arabia rides a camel, not a pale horse." And at the end of life, there is, in the Muslim phrase, nothing but "the whispers of the desert-wind; the tinkling of the camel's bell."

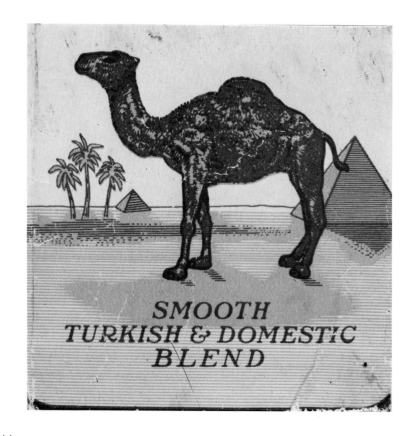

SMOOTH
TURKISH & DOMESTIC
BLEND

CATS

cats and ocelots were good for only one thing:
"Throwing in le swimming pool!" DALI

On this topic Dali dismissed rather lightly the matter of the Halsman photograph and the interference of the SPCA accusing him of cruelty to animals, until he invited their agents into the Halsman studio and showed them the cats sleeping on velvet cushions, whereupon they went back to minding their own business. We emphasized the historic aspects of the photograph, but Dali belittled it in the present context, so I will expand upon it beyond.

In connection with the Halsman photograph, in the winter of 1984 I mentioned to Mrs. Yvonne Halsman that I had looked for years for the original of the oil by Dali that stood on the flying easel. She told me that it did not exist.

What Dali had done was to take a copy of the photograph and draw and paint directly on it. Halsman then made a new negative with the picture showing in it. This ended the mystery of what I thought was a Dali work of that era which I had somehow missed. I record this here, since I am not sure whether or not I entered it in my journal, and the revelation is of historic importance, catalogue-raisonne-wise.

Next Dali related how on one occasion he cut some nut shells in two and then forced them onto the feet of a cat, one half a nutshell on each foot. When the cat, so adorned, attempted to walk he said that at first it had a hard time even to stand up. But when it did walk across the tile floor, it went tic...tic...tic...tic, making "a delicious sound." He added that the noise of the cat trying to walk with the nut shells stuck on its paws was "ideal for sleep." In imagination we all went back to the family home in Figueres where he said he had carried out the malicious experiment.

April 22, 1974 - S.S. France. This evening I asked Dali to tie in the cat to the "sea-phone" (syphon) he had mentioned yesterday at the Julian Levy Gallery. "Oh, is no connection. Is only one transition pour les notes. Le story is dees. In le moment que y yam make le exhibition avec Levy, is see one bust of plas-ter in le store windows. Myself is catch one, et is hollow out where is le mamelon." "Nipple," I interjected. "Si, le nipple, et is cut one round hole dans chaque sein. Et af-ter is putsch inside two cats, et is pulling le tail out les two holes where is les nipples. Et is fasten, et put two little heads of le serpent of gold on les ends of les tails, et is moving like two snakes. Is create one sensation, et is use in one draw-ving on le cover of le program, mais apres no everyone is understand que is le real ee-day-ah (idea). Mais is very amusing."

There are numerous free running cats in Port Lligat. On the stone wharf in front of Dali's house, these stray semi-wild cats await the arrival of fishermen who discard many fish and much fish offal in the sea and on the shore as well. The cats had access, of course, to Dali's garden with the phallus-shaped pool he built in his back yard—phallus shaped with testicles—to shock the people in the near-by Hotel Port Lligat on the hill above.

On numerous occasions with Dali in the garden, he would suddenly reach down and pick a protesting cat up by the neck and throw it in the swimming pool. It would quickly swim to the edge, scramble out, and disappear up the hill or over the wall. Eleanor was always shocked, while I laughed. Dali said the cats and ocelots were good for only one thing: "Throwing in le swimming pool!" (See: Ocelots.)

Phosphene of La Porte — *1932*

I recall Dali telling about the many attempts that were made to get the action photo of Halsman (mentioned in my journal extract) where everything from cats to a bucket of flung water were suspended in the air. He said the cats were finally sopping wet, as was he. There were apparently several sessions involved. At one point some busybody had informed on Dali and Halsman and the SPCA people came to Halsman's studio to stop the artist's efforts to catch everything in suspension—a concept with which the artist was very preoccupied at that time, where nothing touches anything else, as I say in my as yet unpublished journal.

Somehow there was a leak and when the SPCA people arrived, they found all the cats sleeping contentedly on satin cushions. They withdrew in great embarrassment with Dali telling them how much he loved cats, etc. Eventually the pair got their picture of suspended objects, with nothing touching anything else, and symbolizing the great distances now known to separate the particles that make up the elements of our world. This subject intrigued Dali and he avidly followed all the atomic developments of the 1940's. It is little known that the great translator of Dali's *Secret Life* and his novel *Hidden Faces* was deeply involved with the Manhatten Project. Haakon Chevalier kept Dali well informed on neutrons, protons, etc. I do not believe, however, that the artist ever knew that Haakon Chevalier appeared as a character in the dramatic play about the secrecy scandals that emerged from Sante Fe during the 1940's, where Chevalier appeared as one of the participants in the stage version of the various conspiracies.

It should certainly be recorded that Haakon Chevalier was by far the best translator of Dali's writings from the manuscripts. He caught and preserved many of Dali's nuances and meanings which no one else could possibly have done nearly as well. The impact of both the *Secret Life* and *Hidden Faces* stems from, therefore, not only Dali's brilliance as a writer, but also from Chevalier's skill in interpreting Dali's almost indecipherable manuscripts.

The symbolism of Dali's cat photograph is thus totally lost on many people who have no idea how closely the artist followed the development of the nuclear explosion which evolved from man's expanding knowledge of the make-up of the atom. His nuclear mysticism never went over with the critics and the abstract expressionists of the 1940's and 1950's whose "agony" he had predicted in the early 1930's. Dali's flying cats, therefore, still await discovery as a symbol of galactic spaces within the atom where "nothing touches anything else," as well as in outer space.

Satiric example.

CENTAURS

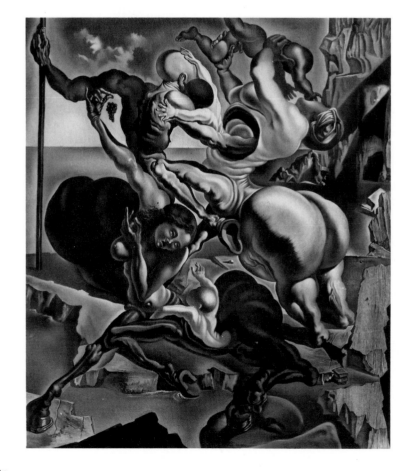

Dali was intrigued with "marsupial centaurs" especially during the early 1940's. "Marsupial" refers to animals with a fold of skin·or external abdominal pouch to house the prematurely born animal where it completes its development.

Apparently Dali coined the idea of a centaur with a pouch. This is well illustrated in two superb oils of 1941. The first is a work called *The Golden Age* which, alas, was destroyed in a fire in an exhibition in San Francisco where it had been loaned by the dealer Dalzell Hatfield, the second was *Family of Marsupial Centaurs* of 1941, which recently appeared at auction.

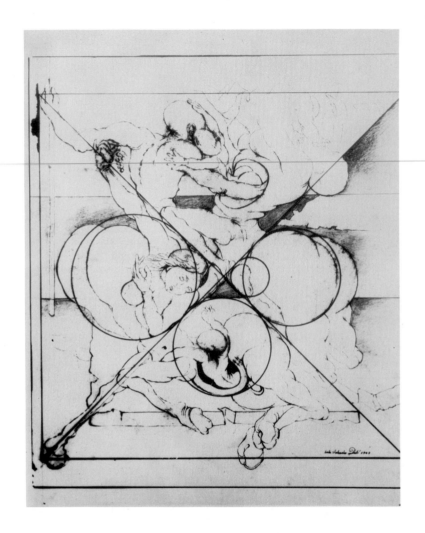

Centaurs appear as details in several works in the traditional format of half man, half horse, especially in *Honey is Sweeter than Blood* belonging to the Santa Barbara Museum of Art.

So far as I know, no art critic caught the significance of a marsupial centaur and it quietly passed into history without being noted as a unique Dalinian concept and a striking anomaly that ideologically went far beyond the paintings depicting it.

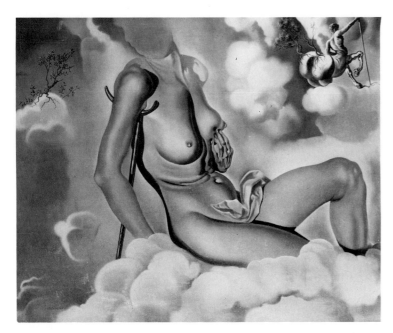

Honey is Sweeter Than Blood *– 1941*

Honey is Sweeter Than Blood *– detail top right*

CHICKEN

The chicken was not much of a topic for Dali's easel so far as I can ascertain. The main recollection of this animal is his reference to it in his famous "emergency speech." People would always ask Dali to make a speech at this gathering and that. When the situation was totally vapid and insipid, and those present not worthy of the master's time, he would baffle those present with his amusing Catalan story of the short legged chicken. He could deliver this Catalonian Classic with lightning rapidity, and always would receive quite an accolade for it, even though no one understood it at all.

In 1987, I got our driver and friend, Bly Mouton who knew this Catalan children's verse to recite and spell it for me one day as we drove from Segovia to Toledo.

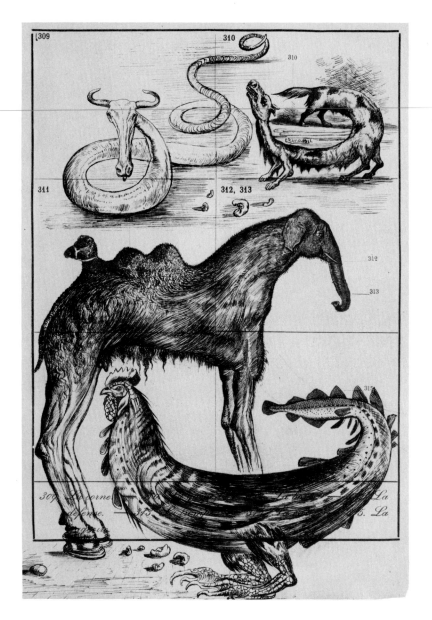

".. Your HoLy UNity .."

53

Dali's Emergency Speech

XICA PICA	(cheeka peeka)
CAMA CURTA	
I BACARICA	
VA TENIR	
SES POLLE	(ses polsch)
XICA PICS	(chix pix)
CAMA CURTES	
I BACARICS	
SI LA POLLA	
NO HAGUES	(no a gaysh)
SIGUT	
CHICA PICA	
CAMA CURTE	
I BACARICA	
ALS SES POLLS	(als ses polsh)
NO HA GUESIN	
SIGUT XICS PICS	(sigut chix pix)
CAMA CURTES	
I BACARICS	

A very small, pecking chicken with short legs
Had six chicks with short legs.
If the mother hen would not have had short legs
The chicks would not have had short legs either.

CHIMERA

A Chimera "is a fire-breathing monster in Greek mythology, represented with the head of a lion, the body of a goat and the tail of a dragon; supposed to represent a volcanic mountain in Lycia whose top was the resort of lions, the middle that of goats, and the face that of serpents. Any similar fabulous monster or idle fancy."

Under this rather broad definition, Dali can certainly be classified as the *only* modern artist who created chimeras on a large scale. The important thing for the Dali student to note in this regard is that from 1939 on, Dali was the ONLY artist in the modern menage who could —or would— create CHIMERAS! Neither abstract expressionism (1945-1955), OP and POP (1956-1969) or the super-realists, etc. of his major years ever touched on mythology. It was a classic concept and thus out of style, with deKooning and Dubuffet. Dali came as close as any modern to classic images that in the least resembled men or beasts, let alone the fanciful creatures of our mythological heritage.

If Dali was refreshing during our major collecting years (1943-1979), it was in his courage in NOT following the Paris and New York schools to their ultimate end in zero art. This was literally the empty canvas showing that modern artists had nothing in their brains, and that it was indeed poor neglected Salvador who was to save 20th Century Art as he truly seems to have done.

CLAM

Dali's depiction of a clam shell in *The Madonna of Port Lligat* is a seldom observed detail. It is at the very bottom of a large canvas and ties *The Madonna* close to Dali's Mediterranean Sea. The shells forming angel wings are seen in the painting with Gala appearing out of them in five different places. This was Dali's first large masterwork and after its preview it was rolled up and went unsold for several years. It was finally sold to Lady Beaverbrook in whose house it went unseen for two decades. It was eventually sold to a speculator and disappeared again for several more years before it was bought by a Japanese collector. Indeed, all Dali's nineteen large masterworks posed formidable and traumatic sales problems involving much agony which we shared with the artist and his wife.

Madonna of Port Lligat — *detail*

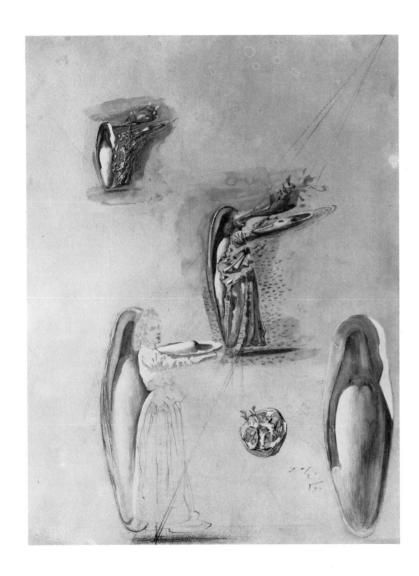

Madonna of Port Lligat — *1950*

The seven references to clam shells in this work are thus virtually unknown, yet they link the work closely to Port Lligat and the sea. Dali invariably ordered little neck clams, especially in New York. With his napkin tucked in his collar, he ate them with a noisy sort of relish, always delicately wiping his mouth after each one, being careful not to disturb his moustache. This image, repeated countless times over the years, is indelibly burned into my mind.

COW

Dali's depiction of cows are few. His most memorable confrontation with a cow was at Caresse Crosby's plantation in Virginia where *Life Magazine* showed them herding a cow into the mansion's living room where the Dalis posed with the animal.

A cow also appeared in *L'Age d'Or* coming into a lavish bedroom and stepping up into a large bed where it massively lay down. Dali's role in this film was minor, but the scene smacks of Dalinian incongruity.

La Vache Spectrale is a bit vague, but is a powerful surrealist work (once owned by Peggy Guggenheim) which I did not have the nerve to buy back in the early 1940's, let alone the money.

CRABS

"Quand y yam one sol-dier," he started. "Where," I asked, "in Gerona?" "No, in Figueres" he came back. "Myself is live in le house of me fader, mais is every day coming in le fort (of San Fernando). Quand myself is soldier, is 'ave les crabs. (Here he used the Spanish word which I did not get because of the terrible noise in the bar. Crab Louse: Ladilla.) Et is spend le whole afternoon pur discover et remove les crabs from down there. (Pointing to his genitals.) Is verk perhaps four hours et is make one pile of les hairs et les crabs. Zen myself is light le 'air, pour burn les crabs, et is arise one dee-vine odor." Here he made a magnificent gesture of smelling, raising his cane and with a grimace explaining how "divine" the smell was. I said, "My God, Dali, how many crabs did you catch?" "Oh, many. Perhaps tventy ou more. Mais in any way, quand y yam boorn (burn), avec les hairs, is arrive one divine parfume!"

CRAWFISH

(SEE SHRIMP)

"Now one crawfish. No le shrimp. No le crevette. Is le ecravisse de la riviere, mais avec one claw comme les homards. Quand Gala et Dali is spent le wvinter in Del Monte is like all le time catch l'ecravisse. How you tell dees, (crawfish) crawv-feesh. Is catch one old wooden boat et is coming in le river pour discover le, le, crawfish, mais only in le spring. Si is eat in le summer is kill. Sue-dently myself is move le 'and, et is catch one e-spine in le finger from le boat. Is one very deerty very black piece of le wood. Is necessary remove le splinter immediately, mais les nails is cut very short et is not possible catch. Is cut les nails parceque y yam paint avec le Prussian Blue. Is poison, is very dangerous avec dees color. Is no find le pin, et Gala is 'ave nossing por remove le splinter, et alszo is very far of the hotel. Sued-ently myself is see le crawfish avec le pincer. Et is pick up et take-ee le claw so (demonstrating) et is pinch so, et is take-ee out le sprinter avec le claw of le crawfish." I had given him the English word claw and he was now using it.

Far from winding down, Dali went on. "In dees time (i.e. during the early 1940's) is arrive many clippings in le room. Quand is retoorn le room, is many piles of clipping et is clutter all in le floor. Is too tired pick-ee up, so is sit in le chair et look le clippings. Is now see le crawfish. Is take-ee up le crawfish and tie on le string, so. Is putsch le cane on le floor, so, (demonstrating) et le crawfish is catch one clipping, et is left, so, et take-ee out le clipping from le claw et is possible read. Et again so, (fishing with the cane gesture) so is now possible write (read) all les clippings mais is no move from le chair!"

(See also *Octopus* where the artist utilized an octopus on a string to retrieve his favorite paint brush which had fallen into the slot in the floor of his studio on the south wall into which he could lower the large paintings so he could always paint at eye level.) As late as 1954 the painting was pulled up and down on a pulley by hand. By 1970 his finances had improved and he replaced the rope with a motor driven hoist. I recall how proud he was at the modernization as he pushed the up button with the tip of his cane to bring the full painting into view! His studio was quite small, probably some fifteen to twenty feet across so it was always difficult to absorb the full impact of the big works. Early on in 1952 he had a canvas perched on the edge of the slot and somehow it got jiggled over and dropped into the slot. When he hauled it back up he was in agony at the prospect of damage. It turned out that, by a miracle, the surface was untouched. It was, I believe, his *Assumpta Corpuscularia Lapislazulina,* a 90½" × 56¹¹/₁₆" oil done in 1952 that fell down the slot which led down to a basement room below in which fishermen stored their nets.

CRETINS

EXCERPT FROM DALI'S PRIVATE DICTIONARY

I will propose to UNESCO that they do their utmost to preserve the cretins, a species destined to disappear.

I try to cretinize people as much as I can, because the cretins are one of my passions. The real cretins are jelly-like, repulsive, completely retarded, full of dribble and saliva. At the same time I always intend to kick society's right foot. If one wants to be remembered by people, it is necessary, when one is very young to give them a kick in the right leg. I find it voluptuous to cretinize people, but also to awaken them.

I always use the word "cretin", not in a prejudiced way, but in the real sense of the word, because when one has fallen in love, he or she almost turns into a cretin, including being silly. This is what happened to Dante and to many great geniuses, who cretinized themselves with the eternal female, until they produced immortal artworks.

The cretinization is of a viscous, jelly-like kind.

I like the cretins (the ones like Velasquez of course). They were the beings that could have contact with supernatural things. But now there are only cretins of bad stock left. I don't know what happened…

As we live in the age of the cretins, the age of the consumer society, it would be lamentable that I should take advantage of the cretins of my time to make more money.

I do not understand voluntary stupidity.

I love journalists very much. They have a great cretinizing power over the masses.

CRICKET

In Dali's *Secret Life* on page 73 there is a tiny illustration of a cricket. It is incorrectly labeled "Grilles" when it should have been Grillon. Below it is another figure — a frog (Grenoville). These little sketches are typical of two superb drawings used to illustrate Dali's 1943 autobiography. These drawings included many animals and Dalinian phenomena. The illustrations of Dali's draftsmanship in his *Secret Life* of 1943 and those in his *Fifty Secrets of Magic Craftsmanship* lift Dali into Leonardo's class as a draftsman, and a modern artist whose drawings belong to the art of history.

EXCERPT FROM DALI'S PRIVATE DICTIONARY

I am interested in crickets because in it's (sic) genetic code they have song much before birth.

Grillon.

CRITICS

EXCERPT FROM DALI'S PRIVATE DICTIONARY

There is the great drama of the critics. The public, the masses, is superior to them. And they always have a better nose.

Now, as I am told, as said by Manuel Brunet, I paint like the piarist reverend mothers and I have to come to the aid of those piarist reverent mothers, because if there is a man that cannot say this, it's Manuel Brunet. What happens is that I don't care a straw what the Brunets say, because I know that deep down they like my paintings but do not dare to say so.

DOGS

"**E**t alzo, quand y yam soldier, is arrive one day in le barracks one very dirty dog. Very oogly. Every day le dog is coming in le same time. Et once myself is catch le dog et is masturbate le dog. Eez very oogly. Very derty. Et after two-three days is arrive le dog again, et myself is take-ee out le penis et insert in le moutts (mouth) of le dog. Is very dangerous, dees." "Also dirty," I said. "Si, alzo very deerty." (This story as related by him in the St. Regis Bar in New York, Volume 16 of my journal under date of April 22, 1974, was substantially the same, but the differences in detail and the animation of delivery were considerable. This telling was briefer.) "Did you tell that one to Parinaud?" I asked him. He replied, "Si, mais is no use. Is create many sings que is no so interesting, et myself is trying to catch les tapes por recouperate les originals."

Dali at the Age of Six Lifting the Skin of the Water to Observe a Dog Sleeping in the Shadow of the Sea — *1950.*

Dogs are seen in many forms in Dali's works. Some of the most fascinating are the double images where a dog appears composed by the viewer's eye from elements of the landscape. The greyhound in *Endless Enigma* is a good example where the greyhound dog is but one of several images. More conventional canines are seen in *Cadaques*, 1923.

The skies transformed into white dogs on a post card from 1932 is similar to one done of cats.

To me, the dog in Dali's world was always more associated with the dog turds that always litter the streets of Paris and New York. Dali would invariably and gingerly touch dog excrements with the toe of his shoe, a dainty gesture that always brought him good luck, for excrement is related to gold he said, though the connection remains essentially a Dalinian secret. The Dali's kept no pets beyond the ocelots Q.V.

Spanish people in general look coldly on animal pets. They seem to have an indifference to animals such as dogs and cats which verges on cruelty. Dali only tolerated the ocelots because they were super hip in New York and always got him attention. They were rarely in his room, as Moore was their keeper. I never saw either Gala or Dali show any real sign of affection for the beasts. Clearly they were just a conversation piece and a useful attention getter during his image building years.

One of the most enigmatic of all Dali's dogs is what Eleanor and I called "The Invisible Blue Dog." We were involved in a negotiation involving the Chicago Art Institute, *The Invention of the Monsters* and *Shades of*

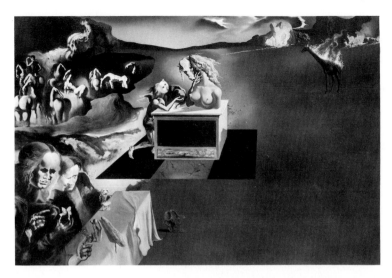

The Invention of the Monsters — *1937*

The Invention of the Monsters — *detail bottom right*

Night Descending. We had the former work in our apartment on consignment, while the latter was in the Winterbotham Collection at The Chicago Art Institute. The invisible blue dog in the lower right center of *The Monsters* was intriguing, but we were perplexed at the other elements in the work. The upshot was that we ended up with *Shades of Night* and *The Monsters* went to Chicago!

In the superb oil called *Sleep*, at the extreme left is seen a small dog leaning into the work and supported by a crutch. The importance of this detail to the balance of the picture as a whole is crucial in a variety of ways from its balance to the abstract questions about the meaning of the images: the dog, sleep and Mont St. Michael. The result is a painting that once seen is never forgotten.

A greyhound is found in the far lower right of *Metamorphosis of Narcissus* as an enigmatic element. During Dali's peak surrealist years, he produced *The Metamorphosis of Narcissus,* one of his top oils of all time. At the far lower right of the canvas a strange sort of greyhound is seen. Here the animal makes no sense at all beyond its placement, again showing Dali's unerring eye for balance in his compositions, its allegorical or other significance quite aside.

During the 1930's Dali was fascinated with double images. Several of his most successful involved invisible dogs which were made up of various extraneous elements. These included a compotier with fruit, his nurse's back and elements from the background landscape which could be combined in the eyes and mind of the beholder to become a canine creature and usually quite a realistic one.

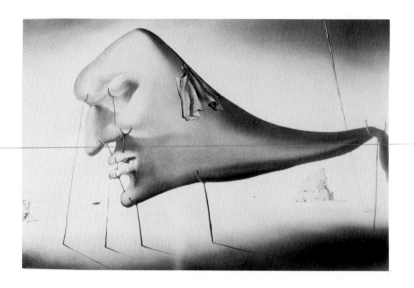

Sleep — *1937*

Sleep — *detail bottom left*

Perhaps one of the most hidden yet most truly spectacular of Dali's dogs is the police dog seen just over the philosopher's hand in *Philosopher Illuminated by the Light of the Moon* of 1939. This work has been recently badly over varnished. It is a dark canvas but the aspect of the dog's head is a truly formidable accomplishment in realism.

In a classic work in Barcelona's Art Museum on Montjuich is a sleeping dog which Dali used in two oils and a pastel. Since the rest of the old master is a rather grim beheading, this reference to the mutt is both selective and provocative. To make this connection links Dali to Catalonia and his heritage in a scholarly and dignified way which was entirely lost on the uniformed mid-20th Century art critics who had not the slightest idea of the painter's erudition, and the reference to the rather grim 16th Century work.

The enigmatic sleeping dog from the 19th century oil titled *"Martirio De San Cucufate"* by Anye Bru seems both realistic and modern. Dali used the dog in several works in his later period (around 1950). Here the hound is depicted as sleeping under the water while a nude child is lifting the skin of the sea.

I was terribly tempted by an oil version of this dog asleep under water which contained a self-portrait of the artist above. To me it was a clear and wonderful statement of a novel concept. To my utter horror when we returned to New York to negotiate the deal, I found Dali had filled the sky around himself with a series of multi-colored balls. I particularly objected to this after thought because the spheres seemed hastily done, full of pencil marks, and overall adding confusion and detracting from the real

Apparition of Face and Fruit Dish on a Beach — *1938*

impact of the great little work with Dali kneeling there in the nude.

I felt this was truly a super-work until the artist decided "to crap it up." I used those words to Dali in declining to buy this final version, and while he pretended not to understand my bold and impetuous position, I stood my ground. At the end Gala got into the act. She said her price for the work was set so high because Dali had spent so many hours suffering as he kneeled in front of a mirror in the nude trying to capture his own pose. So we left the dog of Ayne Bru to his submarine dreams, with neither the artist nor Gala ever quite forgiving me for daring to stand up for the sublimity of this oil in its original form. Who was I to tell a great 20th Century master when he had gone far enough?

Dali's use of dogs had a solid base in *Las Meninas* by Velasquez. His own small rendition of this large and spectacular masterpiece comes off superbly in abstract form in his study of the Infanta in her room. And in a more finished version of this same immortal scene, the dog at the lower right is far more finished. These works were inspired by Dali's fascination with the 300th Anniversary of Velasquez's death in 1960—a historical event that motivated tributes from both Dali and Picasso. The latter, for some reason, also chose to deluge us with a series of pigeons on a Matisse-like balcony. Even today, I felt Dali's little oils, complete with dog, far outdid his friend's best similar, but to me extraneous, efforts.

Two of Dali's most prominent sitters were Jack Warner and Chester Dale. The movie impresario posed with a dog against a mythical classic background.

Endless Enigma — *1938*

Las Meninas — Velasquez

Study of Las Meninas

72

The great collector Chester Dale also posed holding his favorite black poodle. Chester and Maude Dale did more to establish Dali's status in the serious world of art than anyone else. He was a prestigious personality, and Mrs. Dale was a lively and far-seeing art connoisseur who knew the moderns far better than all art critics and most museum directors. Their help in getting Dali's *Corpus Hypercubus* into the Metropolitan and *The Last Supper* into the National Gallery of Art were indeed formidable feats in the world of modern art politics. They saw through the stuntman to the artist, and today the world is richer for their vision. Mrs. Dale once told me she felt Dali's study of their dog showed more real painterly talent than his work on her husband!

The Metamorphosis of Narcissus

Chester Dale — *1958*

Colonel Jack Warner — *1951*

Philosopher Illuminated by the
Light of the Moon — *1939*

Philosopher Illuminated by the Light of the Moon — *detail center*

Martirio De San Cucufate

74

As to critical acclaim, the art journalists turned cold shoulders on these two 1950's portraits, and even the rendering of the pets involved could not move them to report favorably on the works.

The ultimate of Dalinian expressions about dogs as a subject for his easel is found in the invisible dog in the front of the huge oil *The Hallucinogenic Toreador*. Not everyone can see the spotted animal as Dali purposefully concealed it to make a less intrusive subject.

Cadaques — *1923*

Cadaques — *detail bottom center*

Dali seldom undertook a major oil without hiding in it some of his current scientific preoccupations with current events. In the case of the invisible dog the artist referred, of course, to his contemporaries who were lost without true objectives in the mire of abstract art. Here he utilized a photograph taken by R. C. James, an experimental photographer. James used a computer to eliminate details little by little of a spotted Dalmatian dog in order to test the limit of the eyes ability to supply the details mechanically removed. Dali thus tests our optical sensing mechanism and teaches us how the eye can carry forward a partial image and supply the missing details. Here he is utilizing the fill-in power of the human brain in a new and challenging way which is an obvious offshoot of his own paranoiac-critical process for creating new ideas.

Hallucinogenic Toreador — *detail bottom center*

Hallucinogenic Toreador — *1969-70*

DOLPHIN

The Dolphin — *1942*

Dali's 1943 portrait show at Knoedler's Gallery revealed a new and little heralded side of the artist. He was accused of painting his subjects in a ready or pre-made Dalinian setting full of his symbols, and then sort of tacking on the sitter's head as a kind of last minute after-thought. The charge was facetious, of course, but the stunning Dali portraits did momentarily distract a little of the world's attention from the great MOMA Retrospective of his art.

The dolphin in Dorothy Spreckles' portrait and the classic group of sea horses in the background deserve far more credit than the art critics of that day cared to bestow. (They were far more concerned with who the sitter was than with the artistry of the portraits.)

The animal appeared in several canvases of the early 1940's indicative of his bent "to become classic." Remember the art critics NEVER looked at Dali's art in detail at any time. His "behavior" persistently tainted any sympathetic overview, let alone a close examination of such details as his "animals."

Two dolphins are seen in one of Dali's jewels of which he drew the study, but he did not work on them with his own hands as many people still are led to believe.

I recall going to the movie with the Dalis in New York which was based on an intelligent dolphin who was supposed to carry an explosive device so as to destroy a boat and leave no trace of what caused the accident.

As we walked back to the St. Regis, Dali regaled us with dolphin stories, including the attempts of men to have intercourse with them. Eleanor recalls Dali's graphic description of women attempting to make love with dolphins, while Gala interjected a few anecdotes of her own on the subject.

Our stories in rebuttal paled in comparison because they only involved a friend who was putting self-contained heart pacers in the animals preparatory to their use in humans. The problem was how to encapsulate the externally activated devices from body fluids, the very sort of subject that constantly challenged Dali because our own fluids can penetrate almost everything that can be devised to resist them. It was this sort of scientific topic that fascinated the painter who hungrily kept up to date on modern physics. He was always an avid reader of *Scientific American* and loved to speculate on molecules and atoms, especially their structure and movement which was reflected in his "exploding" works.

DONKEYS

During his early period, the artist was often obsessed with donkeys usually in various stages of gruesome decay. He tells of being fascinated by the brilliance of the flesh in corruption. Many times the corpses are surrounded by flies. Sometimes the bare bones are also seen. These pre-surrealist decaying animals were inspired by actual sights of them in his countryside walks, and did not materially impact his later paranoiac symbols because they were REAL. The shock element was probably calculated and served the artist well.

Certainly the two decaying donkeys dripping goo and fluids (added by the artist himself) which appeared in the film *Un Chien Andalou* got the young Catalan off to a striking start in Paris as a total iconoclast. Depicting rotting donkeys, he felt, was the best way to introduce himself to Parisian Society, and as usual he was right!

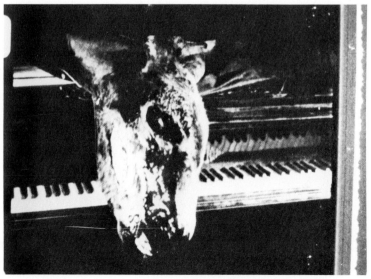

From the film *Un Chein Andalou*

When we first went to Spain in 1954, donkey carts were everywhere and many of the animals were still around. Over the next two decades as chemical fertilizers began to succeed manure, donkeys and their two wheeled carts no longer were a common sight in Ampurdan and thus were no longer major figures in Dali's cosmogony as he never over-worked his shock values at any stage of his career.

Salvador Dali was a born raconteur. Each season as he went from Paris to New York, Madrid and Barcelona (usually starting in early December and returning to Port Lligat in April or May), the artist used a single obsession or a conversation piece. In the year of his Venice ballet, for example, he was preoccupied with soap bubbles. One year it was with bulletism and his arquebus which I had to carry in New York, and another season featured his Ovocipede, a plastic ball into which he climbed and sitting on a suspended seat and using his feet propelled himself around while sitting inside the acrylic sphere.

L' Ane Pourri — *1928*

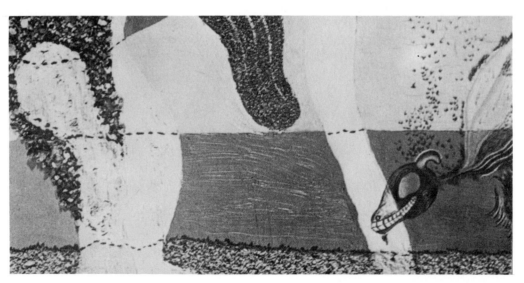

L' Ane Pourri —*detail bottom right*

80

Apparatus and Hand — *1927*

Similarly the King had also a favorite story which he told over and over along with references to his annual themes which ran from cauliflower to rhinoceros. One of his favorite tales was about the Mexican peasant who habitually slept under and in the shade of his donkey in the town square. People would come over to him and ask what time it was as he dozed under his donkey. He would reach up, massage the donkey's testicles and say "one o' clock" or whatever and he was always right! He was a famous local legend.

Finally one day a tourist asked him what time it was. "11 o' clock," he said after reaching up and feeling the donkey's balls. The man looked at his watch and exclaimed "Exactly right! But how do you tell time from feeling of your donkey's testicles?" The Mexican replied, "Oh it is very easy. I just reach up and move my donkey's testicles out of the way so that I can see what the time is on the clock in the church tower across the square!"

Dali made four major attempts to illustrate *Don Quixote*. Each was a distinctive and a major tour de force. It was during this period that a radio broadcaster relating the Don's adventures in a series of talks, closed his dissertation with the immortal words: "And so we leave Sancho Panza sitting on his ass (Rossinante) until tomorrow at the same time." The artist did not quite get the impact of this, as to him the word *ass* in English has two distinct meanings which I cover elsewhere in another book on *La Femme Visible* under the topic *L'Ane Pourri*. Because of this semantic dichotomy, I have made no listing under Ass and stuck with Donkey. It was only late on that I wised Dali up on the slang use of "ass" in English.

Impressions of Africa — *1938-39*

Preliminary drawing for
the etching St. George

Etching —*St. George
and the Dragon*

DRAGON

Dali did a special commission for the Cleveland Print Club in 1947. We were delegated to make the arrangements, and to get the copperplate for Dali. He submitted an initial drawing which was very "sweet" and which the Museum rejected. The painter then came back strongly with a superb drawing of St. George and a dragon. We took him the copperplate on which he was supposed to etch the work. Decades later we learned he had turned the engraving work over to his friend, Stanley Hayter. The resulting print was an instant sellout, and remains a great tour de force, even though Dali was at the time too busy with his image building and commercial assignments to do the actual etching. He may have touched the plate up a bit,

but no one will ever know all the facts in the production of his now famous dragon. This need not distract from the fact that Dali was a skilled etcher working directly on copper, especially after the alloy stylus appeared. He worked on his plates mainly in the morning light of Port Lligat. He did another St. George using Amanda Lear in a late, rather large and dark oil which is hung in Teatro Museo on the right side of the stage facing the audience, but the dragon is far less well defined. And some other "monsters" do exist in various drawings and etchings which are both fanciful and superb.

D U C K

The very early (1918) *Portrait of a Duck* is a memorable example of the young Dali's natural talent. Without such formative experiments in realism and involving trite subjects, he could not have gone on to become one of the extraordinary geniuses of his time.

Many painters found their style and never varied it, from Tanguy, Magritte and Miro on to Chagall. This matter of identity, therefore, was a risk Dali took, probably unconsciously. His oeuvre does have continuity (Dalinian continuity) such as the collar buttons of the Toreador and the hole in the sail of Columbus's ship and the hole in the triangle in *Apparatus and Hand* of 1927. But his subjects and his style are never boring, predictable or topically spiritually repetitive like Chagall who evolved a popular and profitable format/formula, and stuck to it, thus achieving instantaneous identity and ultimately a more solid sort of fame. Thus Dali is always surprising one with some unexpected and unfamiliar image. And it was precisely the freshness of his subjects which set the professional art critics and museum experts against him. Since they could not characterize him or classify his formula, they rejected him as a serious painter.

This is a propitious place to record that NO monograph on Dali's oeuvre as a whole existed until the New York Graphic Monograph of 1958. Thus Dali's early works have never been fully recognized either by the artist's critics or other paid art professionals. Indeed the comment has often been heard about such a still life as *Portrait of a Duck* "Oh, I never knew Dali painted like *that*!" Today Dali's work is uniquely bracketed by his virtually unknown very early and very late works. The brilliance and fame of his surrealist paintings of 1929-1943 thus seem to far outshine those from his beginning and ending years.

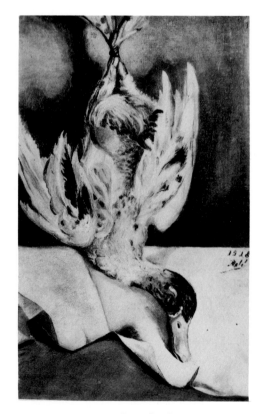

Portrait of a Duck — *1918*

In May 1992 in a nostalgic visit to Port Lligat, I was fortunate in getting Jordi Casals to take a photograph of the tiny upper private dining room with its u-shaped table made out of the native schist. A stuffed eagle once hung on the rear wall on a still visible hook, while the outlines of the eagle are still barely visible in stains on the wall, and just above the blocked in window.

EAGLE

A stuffed eagle was found in the Dali's private upstairs dining room. This long narrow space was mainly filled by a natural stone table made of a slab of the native schist, but shellacked to make it less porous and smoother. The artist always painted from stuffed birds (see Swan) and when the critic Emily Genauer once criticized one of his birds as looking very stiff and artificial, the artist bit his lip and said nothing. Later at dinner he remarked, "Dees vomans is no know nossing. Myself is paint exactly que y yam seeing. Is paint le bird in le studio precisely. Et is catch and stuff one bird express pour paint." As I recall it, this was in connection with the bird in the upper left of *Nature Morte Vivante*.

There is another eagle reference found in a mysterious note in my journal. It reads "In store in Tarragona." This was in 1974 as we drove from Cannes to Port Lligat, with Dali reminiscing about rights and towns along the way. I recall especially the Meter Monument where I slyly got a shot of Dali in back of it taking a leak, while Eleanor copied down the legend carved on the opposite side.

EGG

In Gala's Egg Room in Port Lligat I noted down some of the miniature or toy animals the Dalis had collected and placed on a narrow shelf over the seats that ran around the wall of the room: Four birds, two fish, one skunk, a teddy bear, a rhinoceros; a lion, a tiger, a baby deer, one snail shell - fossilized, a bear with a tiger's head and a puppy in a basket.

The illustration shows some of Gala's little animals on the ledge around her Egg Room. The acoustics—if one stands precisely in the middle of the room—are amazing. Dali popped out of a large egg in one of the documentary films made in Port Lligat. Fried eggs reflecting the eyes of Gala appear in several of Dali's paintings. Pasqual Pesudo, our Spanish nephew, myself, my wife Eleanor seated, Lluis Peñuelas, director of the Teatro Museo Dali, Antonio Pitchot and "Montsi", Dali Museum Librarian and Archivist in the Egg Room, May 1992.

Photo by Jordi Casals.

86

ELEPHANT

We recall going with Dali to see his elephant Susurus in the zoo in Barcelona. He was very proud of it. Later the poor little beast died when somebody fed it an extraneous object. A pop bottle, I believe. Thereby hangs the rest of the story of this anomalous animal.

Dali's elephant related adventures began in earnest with Air India which commissioned him to design a promotional ash tray for the company in the late 1960's. In 1959, he also appeared with an elephant to receive the Medaille de la Qualite Francaise presented to him in the Eiffel Tower Restaurant. Thus the elephant theme was clearly imprinted in his mind. The Air India project resulted in a fabulous object. It was an ash tray that could be seen two ways. Either as a swan, or when turned over, as an elephant!

The artist had already painted the great Edward James oil of 1937 *Swans Reflecting Elephants* which was eventually sold at auction. And following in the next decade came his large oil *Temptation of St. Anthony* with the shocking space age elephants: massive bodies on impossibly long spindly legs. The work was done for a contest on the assigned subject and eventually went from being a commercial to a museum piece. As I recall it, the judges had some real difficulties with Dali's elephants.

He used his spider-legged elephants on various occasions with the their truly surrealistic contradiction being largely lost on his viewers. What they taught was simply that by using the opposite of the expected, one could create a great sensation. Somehow the impact of the giraffe legged space elephants elicited far less of a response than we felt it would. Even his "large jewel" using the thin

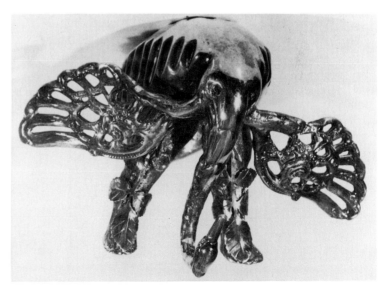

Air India Promotional Ash Tray

legged elephant seemed a little too unusual for many people who just could not accept the physical impossibility here involved. Was it just too ridiculous for unprepared, ordinary minds?

Today two major elephant works are found in the Dali Museum. These are unusual watercolors stemming from the Air India commission, and thereby hangs a major Dalinian adventure.

The truth is that Eleanor and I knew nothing whatsoever about the Air India commission. When one day we arrived in Port Lligat to see our friends, we went at once to their house to announce our arrival. There Katarina let us in, and in the small dining room we found an irate Gala.

Mrs. Dali was wound up for bear. She launched into a voluble and violent attack on us, saying that we had only come to Port Lligat in order to cash in on Dali's publicity stunt! (Something of which we knew nothing at all.)

The objective was to stage a modern version of Hannibal Crossing the Alps. Air India, it developed, had brought a small elephant to Cadaques. There, Dali and some locals would stage an ascent of a mountain, said to symbolize Hannibal's crossing of the Pyrenees mountains for the benefit of the Air India camera men and photographers, with Dali as Hannibal riding the little elephant they named Susurus.

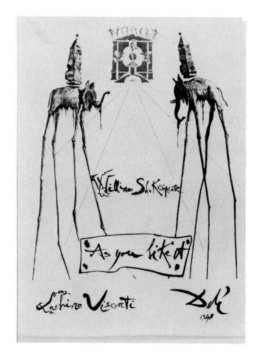

Dali at Eiffel Tower Restaurant

88

Gala's accusation was totally false as we knew absolutely nothing whatsoever of the event, and I was totally taken aback. As she continued her false allegations, I became more and more incensed at the injustice of her charge and the vehemence of her attack. Finally, I could take no more of it. I told her we had had enough of this false implication that we were trying to capitalize on Dali's fame.

I told both Eleanor and Gala that I was fed up and that we were leaving Cadaques at once. I dragged poor Eleanor out of the house and we walked back to the Rocamar Hotel, where Eleanor reluctantly started packing. Soon the word we were cutting short our stay raced over the invisible wires to Port Lligat, and there ensued a long series of very emotional phone conversations between Dali and my long-suffering wife.

Hannibal Crossing the Alps — *1970*

I remained adamant because I felt this time Gala had just gone too far. So despite anguished pleas from Eleanor and Dali, we piled our bags in the car and left, with Eleanor's patience and loyalties both tried to the limit. Thus we missed the "Crossing of the Alps" with Dali and his elephant!

The upshot of the Susurus Air India adventure, of course, was an eventual reconciliation with a kiss, a make-up, and some tears all around. But the incident did establish once and for all, that we were not like the rest of Dali's adherents all looking for fame at the master's expense. As we rehashed our then some sixteen years of friendship, it was made indelibly clear that from the moment we met Dali in 1943, I had decided he was a person never to be upstaged, and that the spotlight must remain 100% on him, and NEVER shine on us. Notoriety was NOT our style and we wanted no part of Dali's image building sort of publicity.

The incident brought us much, much closer to the Dalis, and as the elephant never forgets, so Gala and I never forgot the incident. The true heros, of course, were Dali and Eleanor as peace makers in a unique scenario as we became one of a kind in King Dali's court: someone who had dared to face and stand up to the roaring of the MGM Lion as Dali once characterized his often formidable Russian wife!

Today the Space Age elephant remains a great intellectual challenge of a paranoiac-critical nature. It is not over-popular because it presents simply too much of a psychological challenge for the average mind. By making the impossible come true, Dali has succeeded in challenging the parochial complacency which prevents most people from experiencing the stimulation and fun of his irrational new concept.

Dali's bestiary is thus a constant reminder that we must never allow fairy tales to lose their impact. Indeed his fanciful animals make the strangest dreams seem to come true!

So far, very few people have seen the garden of Gala's so-called castle at Pubol. This walled ancient fortress-farm complex has its own church. It was largely rebuilt by Dali's close friend and former Mayor of Cadaques, Emilio Puignau, architect and builder of Dali's houses. In the walled grounds there are several of Dali's space elephants

Space Elephant

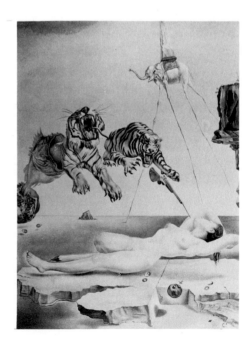

with spindly legs. The realization of these improbable animals from Dali's contrary imagination is, as I have said, always a sort of psychological problem for the beholder. If there is any problem with these surrealist elephants, it remains ours and definitely not Dali's! (The fault, dear Brutus, is in ourselves.)

Dali's anti-gravitational space elephants face inevitable rejection. This is a shame, but it represents the biggest problem Dali survives today: the gradual emasculation, the "cleaning up," of the artist's apparent aberrations. When his "Museum" and its bureaucrats take over the houses in Port Lligat and Pubol, it would not surprise me in the least to see the space elephant's legs replaced with normal ones with the maintenance of the spindly ones cited as being too costly to keep up, or a bureaucratic protest that Dali went "too far" in redesigning elephant legs. It, in their minds, couldn't happen, therefore it should not be. This is a phenomenon we observe in the St. Petersburg Museum as well. I call it de-Dalinizing, the normalization of the master by lesser minds.

Pray that I am unfair in my assessment and that these Dalinian acts will not be "cleaned up" to accord with trite reality! Who but Dali could create —and defend— space elephants? Only one contemporary ever veered near our Dali in this area of constant invention and that was his friend Rene Magritte. Even a casual glance at a Magritte reveals just about all the artist has to say in the instance of each canvas. Dali, on the other hand, crammed his oils full of a seemingly endless flow of details, many animalistic, incongruous, yet withal both necessary and absorbing little details. In discussing this point with Dali, he said that it

was quite true: both Picasso and Magritte created canvases with one major impact. Dali, in contrast, used a multiplicity of details and references, "Pour no becoming boring. Is necessary look les verks of Dali many times."

Then I said, "What about Tanguy and DiChirico?" He shot back, "Is le same. Mais alzo repeat le same eye-de-ah many times. "And Miro?" I persisted, and the master shot back "Morse, you is one ee-stupid man. Is tell many times que Miro is one peasant, one folk artist. Is no so interesting que les udders because is remine too long only on one island. Is becoming very boring."

One of our earliest recollections of Port Lligat is the presence of a huge elephant's skull on the patio just south of Dali's house and outside the library door. It was totally incongruous to us in 1954 in such a wild remote location and remains a Dalinian phenomenon to this day.

Triumph of Dionysus — *1953*

In *The Diary of a Genius* under the date of July 23, 1952, there is an entry about the arrival of three thousand elephant skulls. Dali says "I have five already," and continues "I'll have them spread all over the place in the planetary geology of Port Lligat....There must be no pine trees. The effect would be horrible. Elephant skulls are really what would be best!"

The one elephant skull was incongruous enough, and my last recollection of the skull was that it
  a) Is impractical as a coffee table.
  b) Not weathering very well.

Earlier in his journal Dali says "I love elephant skulls. Especially in summer. A summer without an elephant skull would be inconceivable to me." (Entry July 8, 1956.)

Typical of many quick sketches Dali would make in book dedications is the elephant which is found in a copy of *Dali de Draeger*. His animals appear over and over in these skillfully done, on the spot, spontaneous drawings.

They are so sure, so finished, that I am reminded of the time the Paris forgers were active and fake Matisse drawings were appearing. I asked Dali about which artists in the modern group would be the most difficult to forge. Without hesitation he replied. "Matisse. Is very difficult parceque le line is so sure is impossible for one man imitate." I asked if he could duplicate a Matisse. "Is possible, mais myself is no like make le copy. Pour Dali is always ferst le eye-de-ah. Is more important que le idea arrive, et apres le draw-ving is very easy. Mais in le beginning myself is verk very 'ard pour learn le draw-ving!"

Today, if I were to make any appraisals of Dali's elephants, I would rank near the top those two elephant watercolors found in the Dali Museum Collection in St. Petersburg. These two offshoots of the Susurus Air India project are spontaneous depictions of the coastal Pyrenees Mountains called the Albares. They reflect a still primitive countryside near Dali's lifelong home, and blend in real history without a trace of surrealism. These two works are invariably greeted with the same expressions of wonder: "I would never believe they are by Dali!" and, "I never realized Dali could paint (or draw) like that!"

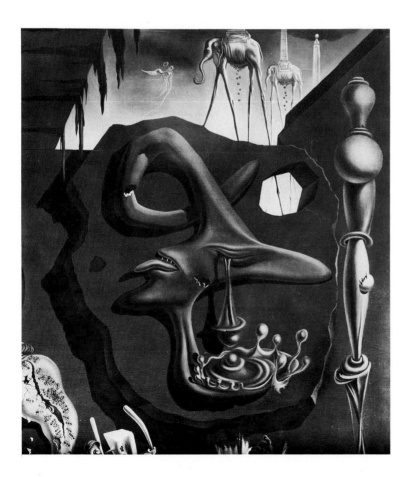

93

FALCON

As of March 29, 1991, I have so far been unable to find one other Dali work with a falcon in it. Certainly the bird in Lady Dunn's portrait is a great tour de force, over shadowed by just one other aspect of this superb example of Dali's artistry which is covered under H (horse).

FIREFLIES

Rosa Salleras, Dali's childhood friend, recalled that as children in Cadaques they would spend hours chasing fireflies and catching them to keep in bottles. Dali verified this was true and quickly changed the subject when I asked if his sister Ana Maria was among the group of firefly catchers. He always resented our having made friends with Ana Maria and considered it a hostile and anti-Gala gesture to mention her name. Over the years, however, the artist knew from the gossip line between Cadaques and Port Lligat that we were always in close touch with his sister — a subject that he remained ambivalently silent about over the years.

We first met Ana Maria in 1954 and became quite a close friend of hers as time went on. (She refused to let us take her to her brother's funeral.) Her dislike of Gala was very real. It was always nostalgic to visit Ana Maria in the old Dali summer home in Cadaques, next door to the Salleras house on rocky Playa D' Es Llanners. [d'es Llanners]

I have never forgotten the evening Ana Maria, Eleanor, and Josefina Cusi made a new translation of Garcia Lorca's *Ode to Salvador Dali* into English. It seemed very appropriate that it should be done in the Dali family home. Incidentally I do not recall ever seeing fireflies either in Cadaques or Port Lligat.

F I S H

Salvador Dali lived close by the Mediterranean Sea for most of his life. Fish from the Gulf of Lyons, the sea and the bays around Rosas and Cape Norfeo and Cape Creus were a big factor in the Catalan's way of living and thinking.

He had a life-long fear of fish bones, however, having choked on one very badly. On one occasion at dinner with Dali and Gala in Port Lligat, Eleanor choked on a fish bone and Dali leaped to go to her aid. He made her eat a piece of bread to help the situation, and hovered over her nervously for half an hour to be sure she was all right.

Dali's fear of choking led to a psychotic attitude toward swallowing. Somehow this phobia seems to date back to swallowing and choking probems which his father or an uncle once had. This was denied by Ana Maria. In the end, Dali had a feeding tube in his nose for well over five years because of his own swallowing problems, making real communications difficult if not impossible.

Thus it was really the painter's fear of choking (loving fish but fearing fish bones) that may have led to his reclusiveness and finally to his physical decline. His inability to talk effectively with the tube going through his nostril and down his throat, certainly makes some of the puzzling events after the death of Gala in 1982 and the alleged communication with the ailing artist, suspect as to their validity. Actually malnutrition was a major factor in Dali's life beginning as early as 1981. After Gala's death and the fire in his room at Pubol, the doctors in Barcelona in 1984 could not begin treatment of his burns because he was too undernourished for them to start the crucial reparations needed on his legs and body.

Still-Life: Fish with Red Bowl — *1923-24*

On one occasion early on when I had come up with a fake Dali, I asked Dali how he could be so sure it was a fake. (It depicted several fish.) He replied, "Is false parceque le fish is no from le sea in front of my father's house," as mentioned again beyond.

Several fine early Dali studies of fish show his knowledge of the local catch. The fish in the still life, *Nature Morte Evangelique* are mentioned in his *Diary of a Genius* on page 30. (Entry of July 1, 1953.)

His *Tuna Fishing* (Q.V.) shows a scene off the coast near Rosas when the tuna were running and which left an indelible memory in his youthful mind of the carnage involved in the bloody business of tuna catching.

Tuna Fishing — *1966-67*

Certainly this aspect of Dali's art (his fish) dates back to the long happy summers spent in the family home on Playa d'es Llaners on the west side of the great bay of Cadaques. The painter's definite nod to Picasso in 1927 in *Still-life by the Light of the Moon* shows a peculiarly fresh stylized way of representing fish with a cubist sense that disturbingly violated the basic form involved. This work has always quietly said to me, "What Picasso did well, Dali can do better!" This is no idle boast as I have proved in my scandalous book on *Dali-Picasso, Picasso-Dali* of 1973.

There for the first time in the art of history, the two Spanish painters are analyzed and compared critically together in the same book. No publisher would touch such a provocative study, so I published it privately. And there you will find the theoretical comparison of Dali's 1927 fish compared to Picasso's of 1923!

Still-Life by the Light of the Moon — *1927*

The Dali still life of 1952 depicting the sacred aspect of bread and fish in a highly disciplined study is a remarkably structured work and to this day there are two titles for the canvas. One is *Eucharistic Still-Life,* and the other is *Nature Morte Evangelique.* In Dali's *Diary of a Genius* the entry for the first of July, 1952, the artist comments: "After having imposed upon myself, as I did yesterday morning, a quarter of an hour painting some glittering scales of my flying fish, I had to break off because of a large swarm of flies...." This is a definite reference to this oil as I believe is recorded in my journal.

Salvador Dali's preoccupation with fish is illustrated by the fact he lived most of life very close to the Mediterranean Sea. On one occasion a very slick painting of fish appeared. I took a photograph of it to the painter who instantly said it was a fake. I said, "How can you be so sure with only a single quick glance at the photo?" The artist shot back with a deadly retort. "Because le fish is no from le sea in front of me father's house." (On another occasion be blasted me with a similar response. I had come up with a superb scene in a kitchen of a bowl, some nuts and a checkered cloth. I said "Dali are you sure this is not your work? How can you be so positive?" And he replied "Because dees sings is no in le kitchen of my mother.") (See also Octopus.)

The superb Dali oil *Mountain Lake* is included here under "fish" because the "fish" is formed by the tidal pool in the foreground of the work. Note that the tail of the fish and effect of the wavelets become scales that create the outline of the otherwise invisible fish.

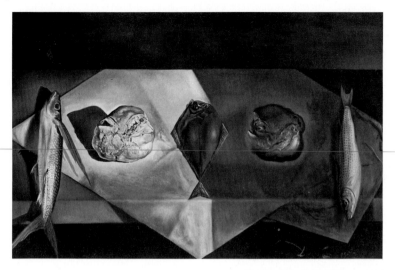

Eucharistic Still-Life — *1952*

Mountain Lake

This canvas is based on a tiny pond found at Requesens, a picturesque castle on a hilltop that at sunset is right out of Maxfield Parrish. In 1954 we were unable to locate the "lake." At dinner in New York, a couple of years later, I asked Dali about the "lake," saying we could not find it. "How big was it?" I asked. He waved his arm pointing to the size of the restaurant (the Laurent).

And so it evolved that a dammed up pond we had located to supply water to the adjacent mountain meadows was really *Mountain Lake,* with Dali never conceding that a pond could be a lake.

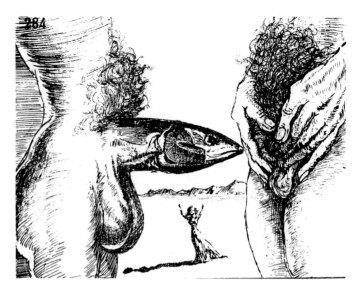

Metamorphosis Erotique, Le Maquereau

Still-Life: Pulpo y Scorpa — *1922*

He topped the matter off by saying that he was four years old when his father took the family up there for a picnic in a wagon, and the "lake" seemed huge to him. But what was burned most strongly in his mind was that his mother wept unconsolably upon seeing the fresh water in the high, remote dry mountain valley, not only because it was so beautiful, but because the first Salvador, Dali's dead brother, could not be there to see it too! The incident started the artist's introspections on the brother who predeceased him by nine months. The obsessions recurred late on and led to his imaginary *Portrait of my Dead Brother,* and all part of the history of *Mountain Lake.*

The fish, the rouget, seen in the *Still Life* in the St. Petersburg Dali Museum Collection is typical of Dali's documentation of things directly affecting his artistic ability which clearly was well developed before he went to Art School in Madrid.

Still-Life Fish — *1922*

Téléphone dans son plat avec trois sardines grillées — *1939*

Imperial Violets — *1938*

(There is another similar red fish which resembles the rouget which I once confused with the rouget. Patiently, he gave me a rundown on the somewhat poisonous and spiny one and warned me never to confuse the two fish again as people would think "que le frien' of Dali is one ee-stupid man.")

During the preparations for the 1939 World's Fair in New York, Dali got himself into a real squabble with the rather stodgy Fair Committee. This was because he had depicted Bottecelli's Venus with a fish's head. They felt it was profane and said so. Dali responded with his famous tract defending "The Rights of Every Man to His Own Madness."

As an observer of this silly travesty, no one brought up the fact that it would have been no affront to tradition if Dali had created a mermaid, a girl with a fish's tail, but a fish's head: a no-no!

Rene Magritte, The Collective Invention — *1935*

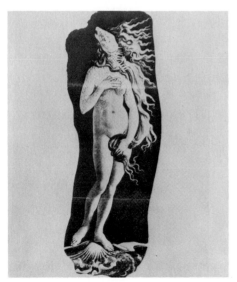

Bottecelli's Venus with a Fish's Head

From: Cyril W. Beaumont
Supplement to complete book of ballets

And much more important in the art of history, nobody raised the question that if Dali was guilty of anything, it was of stealing the idea of a reverse mermaid from Rene Magritte! To me this took the tempest right out of the teapot!

Dali's two versions of his most famous oil *The Persistence of Memory* form an interesting contrast being painted some twenty years apart. The second version with the peace of Port Lligat being blown apart by the atom bomb includes a local fish under the edge of the sea which is not shown in the earlier version. The artist worked on the second oil for over two years, carrying the work in progress in a box under his arm, but with a string attached to his arm.

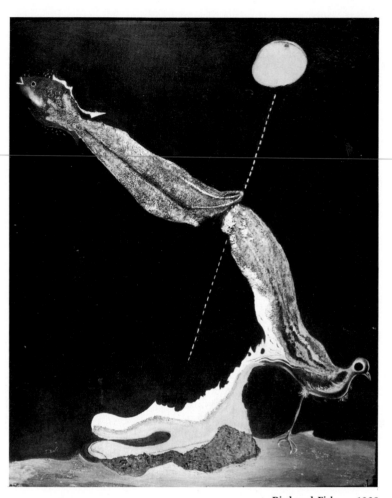

Bird and Fish — *1928*

The Disintegration of the Persistence of Memory

102

We only got the later work after the Museum of Modern Art rejected it as being of no interest to them as a late and decadent oil unworthy of hanging anywhere near its predecessor! It might be mentioned that Eleanor and I insisted MOMA have first crack at the 1954-1956 oil. Accordingly Georges Keller telephoned the Bobsy Twins, the top powers there who said they were not interested in Dali's late works, so we felt free to acquire the atomic version of his most famous oil of 1932, complete with the fish.

First Days of Spring — *1929*

FLAMINGO

"**A**h, alzo one flamingo. Is make one vatercolor avec one flamingo que is make many footprints et is utilize in vater-col-err. Myself is remember very well."

"Myself," however only vaguely recalls this work which I believe once belonged to our friend Dr. Charles Roseman and which disappeared from his house after his death in a tragic auto accident. I could be mistaken on this, but I do recall the pinkish watercolor of the 1940's, and I believe it depicted a flamingo. Today its whereabouts is still unknown.

FLEAS

These creatures appeared in a conversation recorded in my Dali journal of March 22, 1963. It occurred as we were discussing the cats of Port Lligat which Gala would not allow in her house, and the several cats we had in our own home. (We were en route to Carmel and Pebble Beach Lodge when Dali was going to paint a portrait of a lady and her four children.)

A driver with a car met us at the station in Oakland, and we drove off in a sheeted rain toward the south. Dali was very formal and silent, so I made casual conversation about this and that. I asked Gala if she let cats in the house in Cadaques. I told her we had had to put our own cats out of doors because of fleas. Finally, we stopped at a very average restaurant for lunch. There Dali ordered fried eggs and crisp bacon, "for le last time" he commented. We laughed at the skill with which Dali had extracted himself from being made a prisoner of his client, for the driver had showed us the ranch from the highway where she had proposed that Dali stay, but he insisted on the hotel. With an upright finger, Dali pointed to his head and said, "Dali is plan everything very well!"

Then, laughing, he turned to me and asked, "Morse, what is le main key to le entire situation?" "Why, Dali," I replied, "it should be perfectly obvious. It is how well the lady's chauffeur likes you and what he reports." "Precisely," he rejoined, "Is no le lady in dees mais le servant. How you know dees sing? Mais, si you know dees, why is you talk always of fly-ees (fleas)? Now everytime le man is think le friends of Dali have fly-ees!" For a long time he berated me, saying that I always took the wrong approach. First with the famous art critic Emily Genauer, now with this servant and my flea story.

Gallantly, Dali admitted that he too made "mistakes," as he put it. He told of going to dinner one time all dressed in tuxedo appurtenances, except that "after a little relaxation" he got up forgetfully and put on his ordinary tweed jacket! At the dinner everyone exclaimed, "Well old Dali is up to his tricks again, wearing a tweed sport jacket to a formal dinner just to get public attention!"

FLIES

One example of this artist's fascination with flies is found in a sanguine drawing from 1954. It is called *"Seven Flies and a Model."* One of the dead flies is a real one squashed on a piece of paper, 6 × 9". The artist then drew six more so realistically that one is hard put to determine which one is the real one and which are Dali's. It is a real favorite whenever it is shown in the Dali Museum.

There's a photograph of Dali with a fly on his moustache. As I recall it was taken in Port Lligat while Dali was painting in the space between his house and the barracks opposite (actually a stream bed when rains are heavy.) we often watched and talked with Dali while he was sunning in Port Lligat, especially in the days before senile keratoses (or ceratosis) resulted in the doctor telling him to cut out exposure to the sun.* The flies of Port Lligat are legendary in our minds because there were no screens on the Hotel Port Lligat in 1954 and our bedroom buzzed like a beehive with flies. (Nor was there any hot water!)

In his *Diary of a Genius* (Prentice-Hall Edition 1965, page 29 ff), the painter tells of painting his flying fish: "I had to break off because of a swarm of flies..." and continues "...the superhuman problem of painting while being devoured by flies fascinated me and drove me to feats of agility I would not have been capable of without the flies."

As we drove from Cannes to Port Lligat with Dali and Gala in 1974, we said we dreaded Gerona as the flies there were ubiquitous. This was true even indoors in the restaurants. Of course there is the old legend of St. Narcissus and the gad flies which came out of his tomb in the church of St. Felix. The gad flies bit the horses of the French Calvary, routing them. Today the flies of Gerona are not of the biting kind, still they riled us by their sheer numbers.

*Dali sunned frequently and was very tan. I too had a senile ceratosis or dry, scaley skin sores. A Buffalo doctor treated Dali with a fluorine compound that would effloresce the hidden skin cancer. The artist put me onto the treatment as our empathy extended to many areas from the art business to the mundane.

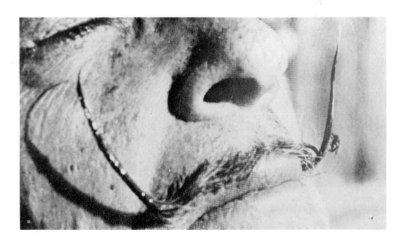

Seven Flies and a Model — *1954*

As we passed Boulou and Beziers, Dali said the flies in these towns were even worse than the ones in Gerona, and that he dreaded going to the latter to accept his stuffed giraffe, a gift from the townspeople for his garden.

The primativeness of Port Lligat in the early 1950's was truly astonishing, and to be with Dali in such an environment was a rare experience, for the tourist hordes who were to replace the flies in numbers, had not yet really begun *their* swarming invasion of what Dali called the most beautiful spot in the world.

There were also some small black flies that Dali liked because they seemed to be clad in a sort of tutu or ballet dress, which he felt had been designed by the famous Spanish dress designer called Balenciaga.

Suffice it to say, the flies of Port Lligat remain a poignant powerful memory for us. For others who have not experienced them, one must understand that they should naturally appear in the works of such a practical realist as Dali.

107

Dali's preoccupation with flies reached a high point with his discovery of a blown up (greatly magnified) photograph of the multiple lenses of a fly's eye. He was fascinated with the idea of multiple direction "vision" and speculated what the world looked like through the eye of a fly.

This obsession climaxed during the late 1950's with his discovery of the ceiling in the Railroad Station at Perpignan, made up of small mirrors similar to the fly's eye, as previously mentioned under "Butterflies".

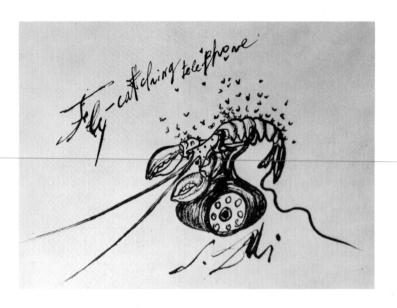

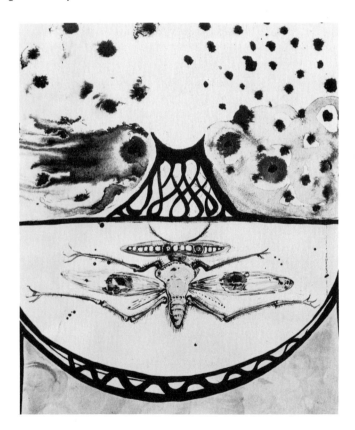

Salvador DALI devant le «Centre de l'Univers». (Photo Claude Nourric)

The subject of flies has always fascinated Dali. Actually he was in seclusion in 1986 when the deputation of Girona paid a significant tribute to St. Narcissus in the form of a large show of Dali's works, many fly related as the catalog shows. I was among those chosen to submit a short essay on the subject of Dali's flies. This is reproduced beyond from the show catalog which was titled *Sant Narcis, Dali i les Mosques*. It is a tribute to the Saint from whose tomb stinging horse flies reputedly emerged, biting the horses of the invaders and helping Girona to repel them.

While Arturo and Gala wrangled with the baggage in the station, Dali would sit and stare at the little mirrors in the ceiling of the small station. Out of these meditations, of course, came his idea that the center of the (his) world lay exactly in the center of the ceiling of the Railroad Station at Perpignan! Geologically it turned out he did have a point. I cannot forget our disillusionment when we finally found this station and how small it really was!

Dali put many flies both in his *Columbus* and the *Hallucinogenic Toreador*. In the latter they turn into helicopters and form a part of the toreador's special sort of hat. Some of his flies in the *Toreador* are very large, and always bring back memories of our first visit to Port Lligat in 1954. There the flies in our monkish quarters appeared in incredible numbers, for the Hotel Port Lligat had no screens at all. I recall how furious Gala was at the proprietor, Raphael Pell, when I came back from Figueres in 1954 with two flyswatters and a toilet seat! Primitivo? Si!

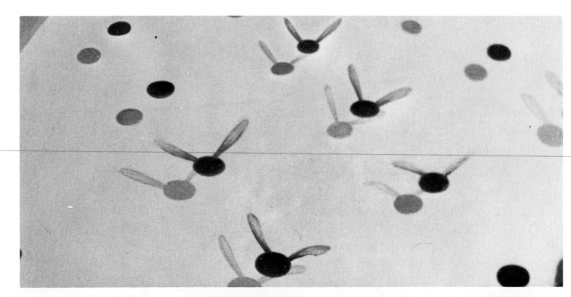

The Hallucinogenic Toreador — *1969-70*

The famous flies of Gerona are frequently mentioned by Richard Ford in his famous 1845 *Handbook for Travellers in Spain*. Las Moscas de St. Narcisco and their appearances are thoroughly detailed by this early traveller who remains by far the best historian of Spain, including the origins and trials of Figueras, "once called Ficaris." No true Dalinian should fail to read Ford's *Handbook* which has been cribbed by everyone right up to Michener, and recently reprinted in readable type by Centaur Press (available from the Dali Museum Store).

Flies have been featured in many of Dali's works and nearly all are reminders of the local legend of St. Narcissus whose tomb we have visited several times in Gerona.

On the subject of flies, the painter was fascinated with the multiple lenses and optics of the flies eye. In fact, in the ceiling of the Railroad Station at Perpignan, Dali often contemplated the faceted little oval mirrors set in the ceiling of the little waiting room. There he announced was to be found the exact center of the (i.e. his) world.

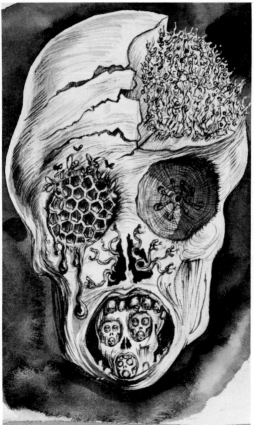

When we finally visited the painter's much touted station and little waiting room (with its very real flies) we were terribly disillusioned by its drabness and smallness, even though the faceted mirrors in the ceiling were fascinating. Only Salvador Dali, however, had the charisma to read the center of his universe into such a humble and ordinary place.

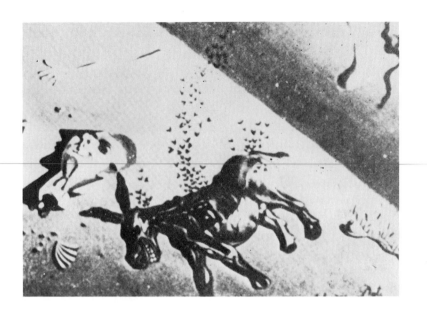

When we told Gala about our appraisal of the Railroad Station in Perpignan she at once related how disgusted she always was with her husband who sat there looking at the ceiling while she struggled with their luggage as they changed trains on their way to Paris. And not being Spanish she was not a bit partial either to flies or the local Saint, let alone her husband's discovery of the center of the universe!

After all, St. Narcissus was Bishop of Gerona from the years 304 to 307, and the miracle of the stinging flies streaming from his tomb took place in 1285, 1653 and 1648! Remoteness in time, however has in no way lessened this still popular legend of the stinging flies in northern Catalonia. The result is that everyone there understands perfectly well the references to the flies in Dali's works. Meanwhile, the broader world still ponders the seemingly incongruous appearance of flies in Dali's cosmology!

My previously mentioned article that appeared in the *Gerona Show Catalog* covers the whole story and is, therefore, reprinted here.

THE FLIES OF DALI

Salvador Dali was the greatest of all the Surrealists. This is precisely because he alone knew all the esthetic limitations of the movement and understood exactly what it stood for.

When Salvador Dali depicted flies, most people thought that it was only some surrealist aberration, or because he is so often (and wrongly) considered «a crazy painter». The opposite is true, of course. Dali was the sanest painter of the 20th Century! And his references to flies proves it.

In 1954 when Eleanor and I first visited Port Lligat the flies were so thick in the little hostelry there that one could not possibly take a siesta. And when we would chat with Dali and Gala on their terrace, there were flies everywhere. The day we left for Barcelona in a taxi (a four hour drive in those days) we proposed stopping for lunch in Girona. «Is very dan-ger-ous coming in Girona,» Dali warned. «Parceque les fly-ees is everywhere. Is much worse que Port Lligat.» This admonition laid the groundwork for the appearance of the flies of St. Narcis which were to appear in his great oil of 1958-1960, «The Discovery of America by Christopher Columbus».

There, in the lower left side of the large oil, Dali depicts St. Narciso who was Bishop of Gerona from 304 to 307. Dali told us that the Bishop was murdered «by gentiles», and that the site of his tomb was revealed to Charlemagne who founded the Sea of Gerona in 786. The grave of the saint was inside the church-fortress of St. Felix, which was named after the Bishop's deacon San Feliu. It was from this tomb that large, stinging horse flies emerged in October, 1285, on September 24th, 1653 and on May 24, 1648. On each occasion, the flies attacked the horses of the invading French with such violence that the city of Gerona was saved.

In America, there is the legend that George Washington, as a boy, chopped down a cherry tree, and when his father confronted him about it, Washington said, «I cannot tell a lie. I did it.» But in America, the school children who are taught the Washington legend, have never heard the legend of St. Narciso which is still told to the children in Catalonia. Thus outside Spain, few indeed recognize the reference to the church and the flies of St. Narciso which Dali perpetuated in his painting.

It is significant that Catalonia should at last begin to realize the mondial impact of Dali's genius even though it has to begin with a story about flies. Today, many countries where Dali lived or travelled, especially France and Italy, are trying to lay claim to Dali and to pay homage to him. To me, as an American, I believe that Dali belongs most of all to Catalonia, so it is fitting that he should be linked to it by a legend that ante-dates the Discovery of America by Christopher Columbus by nearly 1100 years! And all the more so since he introduced the legend of St. Narcissus to the rest of the world as we say in English and not, as Richard Ford the great historian cautions «to be confused with the Pagen puppy».

I believe that Salvador Dali was also the greatest of all the 20th century painters precisely because he led us through the low period represented by abstract expressionism when art had neither content nor technique. Dali clearly went beyond the art of the 20th century and pointed the way to new directions and new ideas for those who will follow him.

Here again the fly is involved, but in a scientific and not a surrealist way. Dali was fascinated by the faceted mirrors in the ceiling decoration of the little railway station in Perpignan. He saw in that modest structure not only the center of the universe as plate tectonics was to prove, but also the many facets that characterize the eye of the fly. With its multi-faceted vision, the fly can see space and perspective in ways we cannot conceive. But Dali saw in it the need to put the third dimension onto canvas. Indeed he went even farther and visualized art in four dimensions.

Having followed Dali's career much more closely than most critics and admirers, it is interesting just how many references there are in Dali's works to flies, mundane though they are. I recall on one occasion when some students of art from Gerona came to the Teatro-Museo Dali. The master was very busy preparing for the opening of his Museum, but he took the time to receive his admirers and even invited them to a drink later in the Ramblas. Dali was delighted when the art students presented him with some flies of Gerona sealed in a test tube. In that ambiance, there was no need at all to explain the symbolism of the legend of St. Narcis. Thus turning to me, Dali said, «Morse, you keep. Is le more important sing, parceque you eez is now 'ave «Le Columbus» et alzo le bishop avec les fly-ees. You is keep pour les archives.» And today the test tube is in our archives, a memento of Dali's humor and seriousness about the importance of the fly in the Dalinian cosmogony.

I well recall how happy we all were when we prevailed on the French photographer Marc Lacroix to take color shots of the perhaps too much neglected painting of the flies coming from the Saint's tomb in St. Felix. This great historical canvas, hidden on a dark wall and missed by many a visitor, is essential to understand Dali's references to flies, not only in his «Columbus», but also more prominently in «The Hallucinogenic Toreador». There flies predominate both the lower and upper portions of the painting. In the upper part the flies become heliocopters, again proving how Dali's mind spans and links events into an exciting continuum which he often described as «the art of history».

When Dali published his comical little book called «Dali's Moustache» with the photographer Philippe Halsman, there is of course a shot of a fly perched on Dali's moustache.

Today, whenever there is shown in the Dali Museum in St. Petersburg, Florida, a little drawing in brown ink of a dead (pressed) fly, it proves to be one of the most popular of all his works. This little drawing dates from the 1950's when the painter found a dead fly, pressed and dried on a sheet of paper in his studio. He then drew six more such images around the real one, and today people still love to be challenged to find the real fly among the drawn ones.

So do not think that Flies and Dali is a facetious subject. It is now time to begin to see what a complex and fascinating mind was Dali's, running across time, and bringing St. Narcis to the age of the Fresnel lense via the eye of a fly. Crazy? No! On the contrary the fly fascinated Dali as it has no other painter, and always with reasons that went light years beyond surrealism. Like many of us today, I am sure that Dali is aware that just as fossil flies are found in amber, when men are all gone, it will be the flies who will survive.

I cannot forget that it was Dali who taught us that future flies will still be genetically connected to those I watched buzz around the artist as I watched him one day in Port Lligat over thirty years ago painting in the morning light on a Pieta for Joseph Foret's massive book *The Apocalypse*.

As an American Dali aficionado since 1942, it is an honor that Dali's native state and district should request me to comment on a native son who relentlessly taught us all about such recherché things as the flies of Gerona —something to which no one in recent memory has ever attached such pervasive importance.

A. REYNOLDS MORSE

Director and President
The Salvador Dali Foundation

DIARY OF A GENIUS

JULY

Port Lligat, the 1st

In July, neither woman nor oysters. *

"Awakened at six o'clock, my first movement is to touch my little crack with the tip of my tongue. It has dried up in the course of the night, which has been exceptionally warm and voluptuous. I am surprised, though, that it has dried so quickly, and that at the touch of my tongue it seems something hard will come off like a scab. I say to myself: "This is going to be fun." I won't detach it immediately, that would be an imprudent waste of the delights of a laborious and patient day of work during which I shall play with my dry scab. For that matter on this day I was to suffer one of the most anguishing experiences of my life because I turned into a fish! The story is interesting enough to be told."

"After having imposed upon myself, as I did yesterday morning, a quarter of an hour painting some glittering scales of my flying fish, I had to break off because of a swarm of large flies (some of them were greenish-gold) that had been attracted by the fetid odor of the corpse. These flies hovered between the nasty mess of the rotting fish and my face and hands, making it necessary for me to double my attention and agility, as on top of the difficulty of the work itself I had to remain insensible of their bites,

116

continuing unperturbed to perfect my strokes, painting the outline of a scale without blinking an eye, while at the same movement a fly clung frenziedly to my eyelid and three others glued themselves to the model. I had to take advantage of the slightest changes of position of these flies in order to continue my observations, and then I have not even mentioned still another fly that insisted on settling on my crack. I could only chase it away by moving the corners of my mouth at short intervals, yielding to a violent rictus that was still harmonious enough not to interfere with the brush strokes applied while holding my breath. Sometimes I even manage to endure it there and not let it go till after I felt it frolicking on my scab."

"Nevertheless it was not this prodigious suffering that obliged me to stop, because, on the contrary, the superhuman problem of painting while being devoured in this way by flies fascinated me and drove me to feats of agility I would not have been capable of without the flies. No! What made me stop was the smell of the fish that was so fetid it was going to make me throw up my breakfast. So I had my model taken away, And I began painting my Christ, but immediately the flies that up till then had been divided between the fish and myself collected exclusively on my skin. I was completely naked and my body had been spattered by a bottle of fixative that had fallen over. I suppose that they were attracted by that liquid because I am really quite clean. Covered by flies I went on painting better than ever, defending my scab with my tongue and my breath. With my tongue I lifted and softened its outer layer, which seemed ready to detach itself. With my breath I dried it, harmonizing my exhalations with the rhythm of my brush strokes. It was quite desiccated, and the intervention of my tongue would not have been enough to

detach a thin flake if I had not helped with a convulsive grimace (made every time I took some color off my palette). Now that thin flake was exactly the quality of a fish scale! By repeating the operation an infinite number of times I could detach from myself any amount of fish scales. My crack was quite a factory of fish scales that looked like mica. As soon as you took one off, a new one instantly came into being at the corner of my mouth."

"I spat the first scale onto my knee. By good fortune I had the highly sensitive impression that it stung me as it stuck to my flesh. I stopped painting at once and closed my eyes. I needed all my will power to remain motionless, there were so many hyperactive flies on my face. In anguish, my heart started beating like mad and I suddenly understood that I was identifying myself with my rotten fish as I felt myself going rigid in the same way. "My God, I'm turning into a fish!" I exclaimed."

"Proofs of the likelihood of this idea were immediately forthcoming. The scale from the crack burned on my knee and multiplied itself. I felt how my thighs one after the other and then my belly grew covered with scales. I wanted to savor this miracle and continue to keep my eyes closed for almost a quarter of an hour."

"Now," I told myself, still incredulous, "I'm going to open my eyes and see myself converted into a fish."

"Sweat was streaming down my body, and I was bathed in the warmth of the setting sun. Finally, I opened my eyes."

"Oh! I was covered with shimmering scales!"

"But at the same moment I realized where they came from: it was only the dried splashes of my crystalized fixative. This was the moment the maid chose to bring me something to eat: toast dipped in olive oil. When she saw me she summed up the situation:"

"You are (sic) as wet as a fish! And I don't understand how you can paint with all those flies torturing you!"

"I stayed by myself, dreaming till dusk."

"O Salvador, your metamorphosis into fish, symbol of Christianity, only came about because of the torment of the flies, what typically Dalinian crazy way to identify yourself with your Christ while you are painting him!"

"With the tip of my tongue, smarting from the day's work, I have finally managed to get the whole scab loose and not just one of its flimsy scales. And while writing with one hand I take the scab between thumb and index of the other, using infinite precautions. It is soft, but if I folded it, it would break. I hold it under my nose to smell it. It has no smell. Absent-mindedly I leave it for a moment between my nose and my upper lip, which is lifted in a grimace that exactly summarizes my feeling of being giddy with exhaustion. A blissful lassitude steals over me."

"I have moved away from the table. The scab almost fell to the floor. I caught it in a plate, on my knees. But this has not effected any change in my prostration, and I hold my mouth in a grimace as if I were fixed like that for eternity. Fortunately the joy of rediscovering my scab has roused me out of unsurmountable torpor. In a panic I start looking for it on the plate where it is just one more brown spot among the innumerable crumbs of burned bread. I think I have it, and I pick it up between two fingers to play with it some more. But a terrible doubt has taken hold of me: I can no longer be sure which is my scab. I feel a great need for reflection. Here is an enigma that resembles the one of the other scales I had imagined myself producing. Since the dimension, the effect, and the absence of smell are the same, what does it matter whether it is the real scab or not? This comparison enrages me because it would simply mean that the divine Christ I am painting of my torment of flies has never existed!"

"This rage contracts my mouth in a paroxysm which together with my will to power forces the crack at the corner of my mouth to bleed. A long red oval drop runs into my goatee."*

"Yes, it is in the Spanish manner that I always sign my mad games! With blood, the way Nietzsche wanted it!"

* Dali never had a goatee.

EXCERPT FROM DALI'S PRIVATE DICTIONARY

I love the fly, paranoiac-critical insect by excellence. The Mediterranean fly delights me. To be covered by flies is a real pleasure for me. Have you not thought in the pleasure felt by being covered with flies?

The Mediterranean flies are very clean. They seem dressed in alpaca from Gibraltar. The flight of the olive fly is delightful. I am convinced that the Greek philosophers were covered with flies.

I put date sugar on the tips of my mustache when I was painting, and a little bit of honey in the suture of the lips, and I awaited the big moment of salivating with satisfaction. When I paint I always salivate with satisfaction. Therefore I waited for the fly to come, to sit on the suture of the half open mouth and then penetrate inside. When I had it inside I closed my mouth and the fly did "Brrrrr...." and I let it go, then another fly, and another.... What a sybaritic thing! And above all, if I did it in the summer, when all of France is bicycling in the "Tour de France" perspiring on the hills, and TV and Radio are talking of the "heros of the trail", and I am enjoying my fly. There is another thing that is also important, that when I salivate and I don't wipe off, a little white crust forms, that prepares me to receive another fly.

I used date sugar, because I was passionate about flies, but the clean ones. Not the flies that move around the bald spot of the bureaucrats, that are repulsive. I am talking about the clean flies of Port Lligat, that crawl around the back of the olive tree leaves, and seem to be dressed by Balenciaga, they are clean and really marvelous.

I look like a fly. I am the center of the world. I am the genius of the geniuses....

The flies have small parabolic lenses in their eyes, that allow me to paint in the third dimension. I would paint my self portrait like the head of a simplified fly.

FOX

Dali's best rendition of the Fox is found in the picture of various animals painted on a special commission for a man who loved animals. See the illustration under "Animals" where the fox is prominently featured in the foreground.

FROGS

Dali then related how on one occasion there was a rain of frogs in Port Lligat. "Very many, very beautiful, very small. Sue-dent-ly is arrive in le sky, et is utilize in one lithograph of Foret."

While there was indeed once a "rain of frogs" in Port Lligat which Dali described to us, the frog is seldom seen in his oeuvre. During the early 1940's, however, the artist did a series of illustrations for various stories by the wealthy chemical plant owner Maurice Sandoz. These illustrations involved many varied animals but only one was related to a frog. This was a mysterious monster and very repulsive. It taxed even Dali's imagination to construct such a loathsome but still "human" animal.

As an illustrator in mid-career, Dali's work with Sandoz was outstanding and was matched in ingenuity and impact only by his four series of illustrations for four totally different issues of Don Quixote. Dali's rapport with Sandoz resulted in top quality illustrations for the Swiss writer's fantastic stores. Some of them have been forged as pastiches using bits and pieces of details from the illustrations to make "new" ones for sale to unwary buyers.

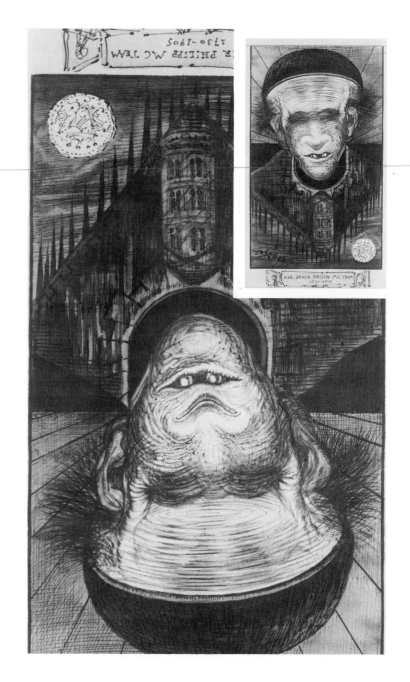

Grenouille.

THE SECRET LIFE OF SALVADOR DALI

Dial Press, 1942, P. 73

"My speeches would succeed one another in a purely automatic fashion and often my words would in no way correspond to the stream of my thoughts. The latter would seem to me to attain the summit of the sublime and I had the impression of discovering each second, in a more and more inspired and unerring fashion, the enigma, the origin and the destiny of each thing. The city lights would progressively turn on, and for each new star a tiny flute would be born. The monotone and rhythmic song of the crickets and frogs would stir me sentimentally by superposing upon the present twilight anguish evocative memories of former springtimes. The sudden apparition of the moon only served to exacerbate my ecstasy to a paroxysm and the megalomaniac tumult would reach such a height of delirious egocentricity that I felt myself rising to the very summit of the most inaccessible stars, the whirl of my narcissism having attained the proportions of a cosmic revery; at this moment a calm, ungrimacing, intelligent flow of tears would come and appease my soul. For some time I had felt within my caressing hand something small, moist, bizarre. I looked in surprise: it was my penis."

GIRAFFE

Diner dans le désert éclairé par les girafes en feu — *1937*

He [Dali] said that somebody had given him a stuffed giraffe. This he had placed in the garden in Port Lligat. "Flaming?" Eleanor asked. "No, stuff-ed only. Mais in any way, myself is many times paint le giraffe en feu. Is many documents que proof que y yam much influenced of le giraffe."

There was a giraffe in the garden of Pubol, a stuffed one that I believe was for a time in the garden of Port Lligat. It is generally conceded that the idea for the flaming giraffe came from René Magritte who had painted various musical instruments with flames emanating from them. Dali both knew Magritte early on and also respected his talent and inventiveness.

122

In Dali's case, the flaming giraffe got him a great deal of attention in America. It is found in the 1937 charcoal *Diner dans le désert éclairé par les girafes en feu,* and in a superb pencil and charcoal drawing of Harpo Marx. It is also seen in *The Inventions of the Monsters* of 1937 in the upper right of the oil in the Chicago Art Institute's Collection.

Both the long legged elephant and the flaming giraffe typify Dali's search for impact and novelty. Such unexpected variations on trite subjects clearly set him apart from such contemporaries as Miro, Tanguy and even

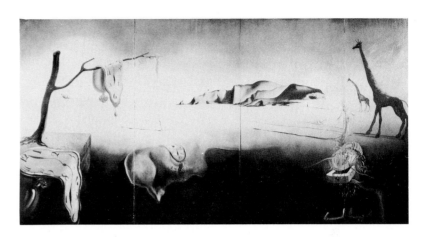

AN EXHIBITION OF OIL PAINTINGS, GOUACHES, WATERCOLORS, SCULPTURE, AND POSTERS

pencil and charcoal drawing of Harpo Marx

Chagall who were all one formula painters. With Dali there was always something new—a fact which kept the art critics continuously off balance—and in a state of shock because they could not trim Dali down to a single recognizable formula.

The giraffe (in fact two) appeared in an oil poster Dali made for the 1939 World's Fair. This large work was one of several Dali did for commercial purposes. Here he made a small study and then had artisans make the study into an oversized painting. To add authenticity to the blow-up, Dali often posed in front of the large work with a brush in one hand and a palette on his thumb. Like his decorations for Helena Rubenstein, these blow ups have repeatedly resurfaced as original Dali oils—which, of course, they are not.

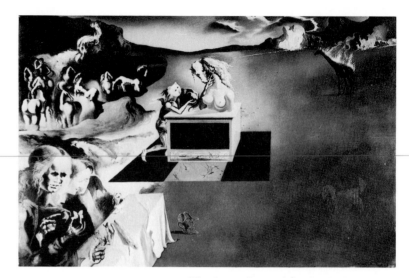

The Inventions of the Monsters—*1937*

GOATS

Dali's *Portrait of Picasso* quite accurately depicted his countryman as a satyr with ram-like horns. The accuracy of Dali's prophetic image did not emerge until the whole story of Picasso's bevy of women came out sometime after his death. This portrait appeared concurrently with Dali's own *Self-Portrait with Grilled Bacon.* I recall trying to buy these two classic works from Dali at the Carstairs Gallery. Both the Dalis refused, and the canvases remained in the artist's collection of marketable works stored away against hard times in memory of their early struggles to find buyers for Dali's easel works.

Portrait of Picasso — *1947*

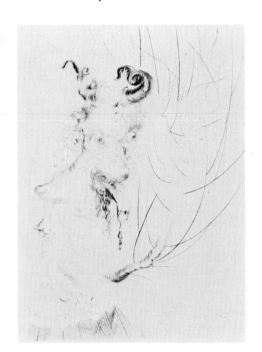

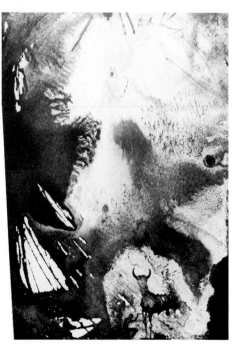

GOOSE

In *Diary of a Genius* under the third of September, 1956, Dali records: "Princess P. has brought to me a porcelain goose from China that we shall put in the center of the table. The goose opens up by means of a lid in its back. I tell the princess divine things about the game of goose that only Dali knows. I imagine that I shall have the neck of the goose sawn off by the same sculptor whom I had add genitals to the torso of Phidias. Only the head and neck of the living goose that is inside will be visible. At dinner time I shall then enclose a living goose in the porcelain one. If it should make a noise we could make a gold hook to close its beak. Furthermore, I think of an orifice that corresponds to the anus of the goose. At the movement of the most melancholic *petits fours* an average Japanese in a kimono will enter the room with a Chinese violin and vibratory appendage which he will insert into the anus of the goose. By playing after-dinner music, he will provoke the swooning of the goose, which will take place amid the conversation of the dinner guests..."

GORGON

This relates to any of the three sisters with snakes for hair "of terrific aspect, the sight of which turned the beholder into stone. The three sisters were Stheno, Euryale and Medusa, who was slain by Perseus using his shield as a mirror to avoid the metamorphic sight. This is graphically illustrated in Dali's illustration found in his edition of *Benvenuto Cellini*.

GRASSHOPPERS

(SAUTURELLES)

Salvador Dali's fear of grasshoppers dates back to his childhood. I determined that it was not a "put-on" one time by bringing a small brass grasshopper about three inches long that I had bought in Paris to his home in Port Lligat. I placed it on the escritor just to the left of the door leading to the south patio in the library.

When Dali spotted my offering, all hell broke loose. He shouted "What eez dees? Take-ee out le óuse immediately!" I quickly stuck it in my pocket, and he continued to upbraid me for several minutes. He said he hated grasshoppers and that he had fully explained his obsession in his *Secret Life*. The artist made it perfectly clear that his fear was real and deeply seated. I suppressed the feeling I had of trying to say it was just a joke — for it was certainly clear that it was one he would not appreciate. He continued his chastisement of me for being so foolish for at least five minutes. The incident left no doubt in my mind about his position versus grasshoppers.

Profanation of the Host — *1929*

127

While he had exorcised himself of his fears by painting grasshoppers, they remained to the end real monsters— ugly and frightening, just as when Rosa Salleras had put one down his neck as a child. She said the reaction was violent indeed, and while the other children would still tease him with grasshoppers, she never did so again, despite the urgings of the other young friends in their group in Cadaques.

In his paranoiac-critical interpretations he often depicted the creatures clinging to the front of a face seen from the side. The grasshopper in *The Great Masturbator* of 1929 was by far the most disturbing as it had ants and eggs clinging to its own striped belly. The insect is also seen in Dali's surrealist portrait of Paul Eluard.

portrait of Paul Eluard

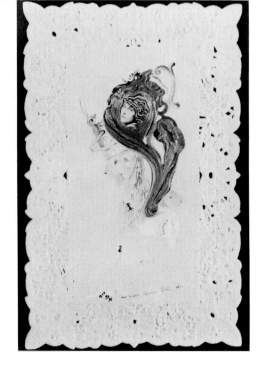

Dali's long-nosed faces, of course, are based on the outline of the great masturbator rock on Cape Creus which seems to be an anguished long-nosed face pressing against the ground. This "head" is a geological feature and yet it is one closely related to his grasshoppers, as well as to *The Persistence of Memory* and other major works where no grasshoppers are featured, but the sort of faces are seen.

EXCERPT FROM DALI'S PRIVATE DICTIONARY

What gave me the greatest scare are grasshoppers. They possess a great mystic suffering. When children torture them, their capacity to suffer is incalculable. They can live for a long while with their head flattened like a tortilla and hold on to you with strength. I have lived my childhood being frightened by grasshoppers. The grasshopper is a demonic animal with a suffering horse's face.

The grasshopper, a very slim fountain pen.

The Secret Life of Salvador Dali

One morning I had caught a very slimy little fish, called a "slobberer" because of this. I pressed it very hard in my hand so as to be able to hold it without its slipping away, and only its small head emerged from my hand. I brought it close to my face to get a good look at it, but immediately I uttered a shrill cry of terror, and threw the fish far away, while tears welled into my eyes. My father, who was sitting on a rock nearby, came and consoled me, trying to understand what had upset me so. "I have just looked at the face of the 'slobberer,'" I told him, in a voice broken by sobs, "and it was exactly the same as a grasshopper's!" Since I found this association between the two faces, the fish's and the grasshopper's the latter became a thing of horror to me, and the sudden and unexpected sight of one was likely to throw me into such a spectacular nervous fit that my parents absolutely forbade the other children to throw grasshoppers at me, as they were constantly trying to do in order to enjoy my terror. My parents, however, often said, "What a strange thing! He loved them so much before!"

Daybreak

The Great Masturbator — *1929*

129

G U L L

(GABIOTA), Sea-Gull Q.V.

When Dali was painting his large canvas *Tuna Fishing* he related that he had just averted a major crisis. Under Sea Gull, I relate how Arturo had come to the studio to deliver a message when he happened to look at the painting. It was wrong, the faithful retainer said. The sea gull carrying the fish was incorrectly shown holding the fish by the tail. The gull always held the fish by the head, Arturo said, so that when the bird tossed the fish into the air to eat it, it would fall head first into the bird's gullet. So the artist altered the picture. On reflection we all agreed Arturo was right because obviously the scales of the fish would prevent it from going down if it were swallowed tail first. Eleanor commented that with the Master's usual acute observation to details, she was surprised he had not shown it right in the first place. I felt it was good that it was Arturo who had spotted the mistake, for Dali was not one to accept criticism of a work in progress from anyone else but his houseman and Sr. Isidro Bea, his faithful studio aide. It was Bea who projected Dali's sketches up to the full scale of the painting from Dali's small preliminary drawings. Bea was active as a projectionist for stage sets in Barcelona and did a lot of work on such huge pieces as the crazy backdrops used in Dali's sets for "The Roman Lady and the Gladiator" staged in Venice. As a collaborator and close friend, Bea often helped Dali in the studio as an assistant in blowing up Dali's sketches to the desired size, while Dali remained the only source of the ideas involved, along with executing most of the finer details. In no way did Sr. Bea act as other than a close friend and essential studio assistant.

HEDGEHOG

(See Porcupine, Maggots and Worms)

Dali's *Secret Life* contains many details of his animalistic experiences. Since nobody can tell it like Dali, there follows his description of a hedgehog together with its dissolution. The illustration he made for his book on page 94 shows not only the cadaverous worms, but also the ants attracted to the dead beast. This text should be compared to that given under Porcupine which we must assume to be in error for my own experiences in Colorado with porcupines tell me that a young boy in his right mind would never adopt a porcupine as a pet.

"The large hedgehog, which I had been unable to find for more than a week, and which I thought had miraculously escaped, suddenly appeared to me in a corner of the chicken-coop behind a pile of bricks and nettles: it was dead. Full of repulsion I drew near it. The thick skin of its bristle-covered back was stirring with the ceaseless to-and-fro movement of a frenzied mass of wriggling worms. Near the head this crawling was so intense that one would have said that a veritable inner volcano of putrefaction was at any moment about to burst through this skin torn by the horror of death in an imminent eruption of final ignominy. A slight trembling accompanied by an extreme feebleness seized my legs and delicate cold shudders rising vertically along my back spread fanwise in the back of my neck, from which they fell back, branching outward through my whole body like a veritable burst of fireworks at a feast of the apotheosis of my terror. Involuntarily I drew still closer to this foul ball which continued to attract me with a revolting fascination. I had to get a really good look at it."

"But a staggering whiff of stench made me draw back. I ran from the chicken coop as fast as my legs would carry me; coming close to the linden blossoms I took a deep breath of the fragrance with the idea of purifying my lungs; but presently I retraced my steps to continue the attentive observation of my putrefied hedgehog. During the time that I remained near it I completely stopped breathing, and when I could no longer hold my breath I dashed off again toward the linden blossom pickers, who by this time had accumulated great piles humming with bees. I took advantage of these breathing spells to pour out the dark water of my glance into the sunny well of Dullita's celestial eyes."

HERMIT CRAB

"Now is Bernard l'Hermit. Is verk in le shell. Is encrusted wiz precious stones." Then he related how one time he managed to transfer a hermit crab from one shell to another by placing an empty shell near the one inhabited by a hermit crab. The loud music and the terrific noise level in the bar of the S.S. France interfered with my getting all the details of this story fixed in my mind. It should be remembered that the main substance of this book originated with Dali and our many conversations with him which I recorded in a separate notebook kept for *Animal Crackers*, and also in my journal. It was thus actually many years in the writing, plus a long hiatus until I could get rid of a major problem in the Dali Museum and devote myself to my main purpose of presenting Dali as a wonderful jovial friend who entirely changed the course of Eleanor's and my lives.

HORSES

"Is now arrive one stuff-ed horse. Is putsch in le cast-tel in Pubol, le cast-tel of Gala, in le barn. Is possible look down in le living room, et quand is illumine, is appear le horse. Myself is draw le horse more times que y yam knowing. Le most important is le horse in le Campodoglio que y yam expline quand you is in Rome in le night. Is tell que le naz (nose) is very long. Le horse of Marcus Aurelius is le most beautiful of all."

The selection of the animal illustrations for the brief summary of Dali's use of the horse in his cosmology are purposely separated out and follow the introductory text as a group.

To do Dali's horses justice, however, would require a book devoted entirely to depictions of this one animal as the selections that follow can only begin to indicate.

We recall sitting in Pubol with the Dalis in 1970 and looking down through the glass topped "Fixed" coffee table to the stuffed horse in the basement barn. This same "animal" I believe turned up as a gift to Dali and somehow found its way to Dali's second floor suite in the Meurice Hotel in Paris where it was totally incongruous. Later we went downstairs to look at the two tombs prepared there for our friends. The memory is painful today, because the inseparable pair belong together in eternity as in life. So Gala sleeps in Pubol alone and Dali is in a tomb just off the men's room of the Teatro Museo, and so located that visitors to the old stage level above daily walk on the slab over the master's grave. In fact I felt especially uncomfortable in October 1990 sitting through a concert in the Teatro in a chair two legs of which rested on Dali's grave!

The horse in Dali's bestiary is without doubt the most often depicted of all his animals, both in drawings and oils. From the early clean lined horse drawing done as an illustration for the book *L'Oncle Vincents* in 1926 on to his splashy series of watercolors on famous historical horses made some sixty years later expressly for reproduction, Dali's artistry often veered near the old masters.

In many instances horses appear on his canvases both on his serious and commissioned portraits as small details apparently unrelated to the rest of the scene. But do not underrate these bits of cavalry for they always somehow fit and turn out to have a distinct purpose in the composition and the mood of the piece.

The Broken Bridge and the Dream — *1945*

134

In the great portrait of Lady James Dunn on horseback holding a falcon, there is one detail that towers even over his sheer artistry seen in the figure and the animal. It proves Dali's total mastery of his medium and his subject. Note the horse's eye. In just one quick dash or daub of white pigment, Dali makes a slick, superb painting into a great tour de force. Only a master painter would dare to undertake such a spontaneously critical brush stroke. Without it, the portrait would remain great, but with the quick dot of white in the horse's eye, it becomes a true masterpiece and irrefutable proof of his artistry.

Dali's early attempts at a double image in his *Allegory of Sunset-Air* around 1930 are a fascinating metamorphosis. His works in this vein went totally unappreciated, and were

Portrait of Lady James Dunn

135

clearly well over the heads of his surrealist consorts. This was for only one reason. The transformation was the epitome of his Surrealism, but being SURREALISTS they totally missed Dali's contribution both actual and potential to their wobbly movement, and one ill-timed for in the Great Depression of 1930 the world was in no mood for art without discernable reason to which one could cling in a global slump.

Many of Dali's horse drawings rival Leonardo, Dürer and the masters of the past. Their inherent draftsmanship make their surrealist elements part of the art of history, and do so in such a classical style that the result is no art critics have ever felt it necessary to comment on these "classic" works.

Dali's use of the horse is by no means conventional or traditional. The spindly-legged horse in *Temptation of St. Anthony* is the antithesis of the flying one in *William Tell* of 1930. And both steeds, of course, stem from the one seen in the great 1890's rococo auditorium in Barcelona where Dali often went as a child and young man. It is up near the ceiling on the right of the stage, and is a distinctive feature of the ornate decor of the splendid Palace of Catalan Music.

It is no coincidence that in Dali's great oil *The Battle of Tetuan* in the upper left, the over powering torso of the general's horse is precisely that seen in the Palace of Catalan Music to the right of the stage and up near the ceiling! This re-use of Dalinian symbols is called Dalinian Continuity precisely for the reason illustrated here: it shows Dali's treatment of his various obsessions at all the different stages of his development.

Temptation of St. Anthony — *1946*

William Tell — *1930*

136

Horse in rococo auditorium in Barcelona

Study for the Battle of Tetuan

The Battle of Tetuan

No better paranoiac-critical manifestation is found than the *Lion, Horse and Invisible Sleeping Woman* which was destroyed by protestors at the showing of *L'Age d'Or* in Paris in 1930. In France they attacked Dali's ideas. In America, they simply ignored the concept that there might be real substance in his madness that was not mad!

Chevalier de la Morte of 1935 is a moody nod toward *The Isle of the Dead* by Arnold Boecklin. It is also one of the many Dali oils we had on consignment in our home over the years which we decided not to buy for various reasons.

Lion, Horse and Invisible Sleeping Woman

138

Chevalier de la Morte — *1935*

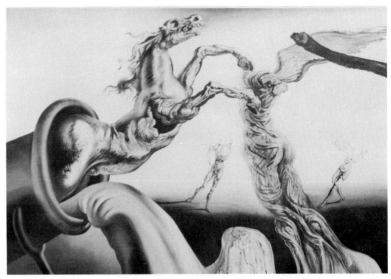

Daddy Longlegs of the Evening…Hope! — *detail top left*

Daddy Longlegs of the Evening…Hope! — *1940*

By far the most significant Dali horse historically is that seen in *Blind Horse Biting a Telephone* of 1938. This forceful canvas was Dali's single nod towards Picasso's overpowering *Guernica* which is now enshrined in Madrid in the Reina Sofia Museum. The *Blind Horse* just could be the most important work historically in the collection of New York's Museum of Modern Art. But will the art bureaucrats there ever admit it?

I place *Blind Horse* above even the great masterwork *Santiago el Grande* of 1957 even though we were on the scene as the latter huge canvas evolved. *Santiago el Grande,* of course, is deeply involved in the legend underlying The Milky Way, the pilgrims' route to Santiago de la Compostela, and the miraculous appearance of St. James who rode out of the sea on his steed to help route the Saracens.

Blind Horse Biting a Telephone — *1938*

Santiago el Grande — *1957*

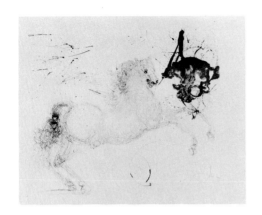

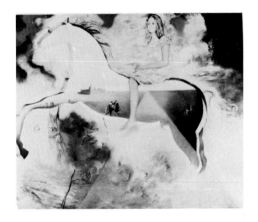

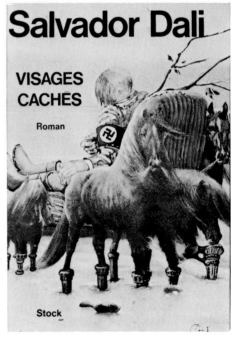

In 1962 Dali's interest in horses intensified as he began work on *The Battle of Tetuan*. Here a photograph of Arabic horsemen in *Life*, I believe, was the model for the galloping animals in the masterwork where Dali really did the horse proud. We were particularly taken with the powerful little *Study for the Battle of Tetuan*, a small pinkish panel about 7¼″ × 9¼″ which Gala refused to sell and which now is in Spain's collection somewhere.

The culmination of Dali's long fascination with the horse came with *Copy of a Rubens Copied After a Leonardo* of 1979. This small oil (18 × 24 mm) was indelible proof that the painter's talent was **NOT** yet waning as many feared. The canvas overwhelmed us when we saw it in the Pompidou Show but we did not dare to broach the question of acquiring it with Gala because she was becoming obsessed with her husband's failing health and his confusions, still unexplained.

Autumn Sonata — *1945*

There can be little question that of all the animals in Dali's bestiary and allegorical references, the horse was probably the most represented (not counting ants, of course). The little groups of the rearing animals seen in such works as the portrait of *Count Theo Rossi* or *The Apotheosis of Homer* remain a distinctive aspect of his serious oils which always set them apart from anything else on the otherwise very drab contemporary scene of 1943-1973.

But above all, remember, the young Dali in the splendid Palace of Catalan Music and the decorative horse in flight on the right of the stage and just under the ornate ceiling. The impression of Montaner's aerial horse never left the artist. It is totally incongruous that a horse should fly out of either a ceiling or a cypress tree. This "contrary to expectation" technique carried itself over to the horses and elephants precariously supported on improbably spindly legs and which became a viable and valuable part of Dali's little explored formula for his special sort of success and fame. He always went in the opposite direction of the crowd both physically and intellectually. His system of opposites was a workable one, however, and today we can accept a flying horse. Thanks to Montaner and to Dali's ability to generate new ideas even as a lad in Barcelona!

Perhaps the real key to Dali fascination with horses began with the famous equestrian statue of Marcus Aurelius in the Campodoglio in Rome. There Dali had his studio in Lord Bernier's apartment in the late 1930's. This overlooked the ruins to the south, and to get into the building one has to pass the Aurelius horse.

Portrait of Count Theo Rossi

Statue of Marcus Aurelius
in the Campodoglio in Rome

144

One evening in 1954 after dinner, Dali took us to the Campodoglio and gave Gala, Eleanor and myself a half hour lecture on horses and why this one of Marcus Aurelius was the epitome of his many interpretations of the horse. He pointed out the exaggerations purposely done for emphasis, and the esthetic reason for the obvious disproportions which included the size of the rider's foot.

Afterwards we walked down the Roman steps, with our heads spinning from Dali's analysis of this superb statue. The experience changed everything we thought we knew about the anatomy of the horse and it would be hard to depict one effectively without having just meditated on Marcus Aurelius' superb animal! Never for an instant should anyone try to criticize Dali's horses without having the art lesson Dali gave us that happy night in Rome! It was but one of many occasions when the master took the time to straighten out our thinking so that we could learn to tell the vital difference between the history of art and the art of history.

Among Dali's most spectacular achievements was his unique work as an illustrator for Don Quixote de la Mancha by Cervantes. This should come under the heading of horses because of the artist's frequent treatment of Rozinante, Don Quixote's lanky horse. (Sancho Panza's beast is called simply "his ass"). In 1946 appeared the Random House Pocket Book edition of *Don Quixote*. (This was followed in 1979 by a larger format edition from Abbeville Press, New York.) In 1957 Dali produced another set of illustrations from Don Quixote. This appeared in an oversized format published by Emecé Editores S.A. of Buenos Aires. Then in 1964-65 the artist produced a third series of Don Quixote illustrations which appeared serially in the Italian magazine *Tempo* from September 1964 to April 14, 1965.

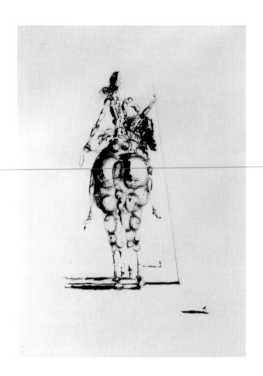

The painter's fourth set of Don Quixote illustrations was done in Paris by Josef Foret. It consisted of fifteen original lithographs done on stone and comprises more than half of the some twenty-three or so original genuine lithographs that Dali produced. It appeared on December 13, 1957 in Paris and rapidly sold out.

We often discussed original lithographs done on stone with the artist. It was too much work for him, as the stones were impractically bulky. He went to zinc plates for a while, and when his nemesis Moore appeared he stopped making original lithographs entirely and went to commissioned watercolors or gouaches for which he charged the client $100,000. This began around 1963. These watercolors were made expressly for reproduction in limited editions which he would sign in the agreed on number. These works are not to be confused with the later reproductions of his famous oils, carrying forged signatures and sold at high prices as art investments by his gangster exploiters.

This extraordinary series of achievements, of course, are full of variations treating the woeful knight's horse Rozinante and also many versions of Sancho Panza's ass. Each of these suites involving many animal illustrations is done in various mediums. So far not one Dali scholar has even mentioned this incredible achievement of the Spanish artist who produced not one but four distinct illustrated editions of what is Spain's most famous novel. Today we

  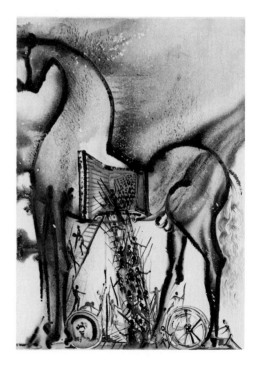

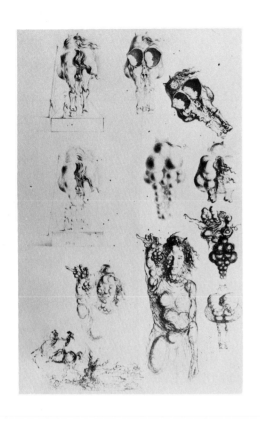

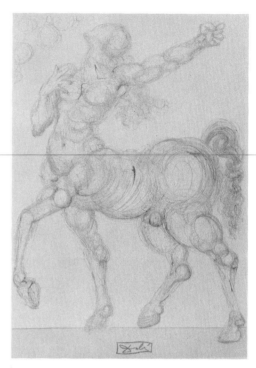

badly need a scholarly and definitive book on Dali as an illustrator to replace a rather hastily one done in Barcelona some time ago, and which is far from definitive.

It is also interesting that several fake drawings containing horses have surfaced. These pastiches draw on various Dalinian details such as the horse as rendered in circles. They prove just one thing. That is how truly superb was Dali's draftsmanship which probably peaks in his horse drawings.

INSECTS

"**A**h, one udder. Is arrive in Figueres in la primavera, each spring, one insect avec one long nose pour catch le honey in les flowers." "A humming bird?" I asked. "No, one insect avec le long proboscis. Et in le moment of arrive myself is sit between two girls et is take-out le sex pour masturbate. (And here he made a gesture of holding his penis with one hand and pointing to its head in his fist with the end of his cane.) In any way le insect is arrive in le same moment pur take-ee out le drop from le end of le sex. Myself is very afraid quand le insect is arrive so close of me sex. Is possible kill Dali. Is no let le bug suck le penis parceque si Dali is kill by one insect, everybody is tell que y yam absolutely crazy!"

There are many categories of insects in Dali's bestiary. One of the most amusing was the watercolor portrait of Roosevelt and Lincoln, made up out of details of various insects. This 1942 work took many by surprise and it long sought a buyer. There is a legend that in California Dali once painted eyes complete with false eyelashes glued on the backs of roaches and released them in the Del Monte Lodge in California in the 1940's to astound some revelers as they returned to the hotel in the early morning.

My notes include mention of *Morros de con* and *Coléoloptère* (beetle) and also of a mimetic insect which had the appearance of a thorn on the stem of a rose. And flies, of course, which were everywhere in Port Lligat, including dead ones on his palette and in boxes, etc., among the litter of his studio. Sabater, I believe, caught one in a photograph on Dali's moustache, much to the artist's delight; and Halsman took a similar photograph but posed. There are also the scorpions in *L'Age d'Or,* as well as ants and spiders which should have categories all their own in any analysis of Dali's insect world of animals and creatures of all sorts real, fabled or allegorical.

Certainly, the praying mantis received a great deal of the artist's attention, especially since the painter cottoned to the legend that the female insect ate the male after copulation—"a nuptial meal." Dali's *Tragic Myth of Millet's Angelus* was an obscure book which I tried to spark up a little in 1986 when Jean-Jacques Pauvert kindly gave the Dali Museum permission to bring out a new edition. In our present context, the main point to record is that an insect expert once and for all states "in natural conditions the nuptial meal of the praying mantis does not exist." I have since ascertained that the legend Dali loved of the post coital meal does have a basis in fact. It arose because when the mantises are in captivity this cannibalism actually **DOES** occur, but not in the wild natural habitat, so there was a basis for Dali's story after all.

Previous reference has been made to the mimetic insect which disguises itself so as to appear to be a leaf and part of a plant that grows on Cape Creus and around Cadaques. It requires some elaboration because it was a subject dear to the painter's heart. Indeed Dali devotes several paragraphs of his *Secret Life* of 1943 to it on pages 68 and 69. Since no one can describe a Dalinian obsession better than the artist himself, there follows the piquant text relating to his leaf-insect:

"To be sure, I did not advance in that painful upward climb of arithmetic, I did not succeed in the sickly and exhausting calculation of multiplication. On the other hand I, Salvador Dali, at the age of nine, discovered not only the phenomenon of mimesis*, but also a general and complete theory to explain it!"

"At Cadaques that summer I had observed a species of plant that grows in great profusion along the seashore. These plants when seen at close range are composed of small, very irregular leaves supported on stems so fine that the slightest breath of air animates them in a kind of constant quivering. One day, however, some of these leaves struck me as moving independently of the rest, and what was not my stupor when I perceived that they walked! Thereupon I isolated that curious and tiny leaf-insect from the rest to observe it at leisure and examine it minutely. Seen from behind it was impossible to distinguish from the other leaves among which it lived, but if one turned it over, its abdomen appeared no different from that of any other beetle, except for its legs which were perhaps unusually delicate and were in any case invisible in their normal position. The discovery of this insect made an inordinate impression on me for I believed I had just discovered one of the most mysterious and magic secrets of nature.† And there is no shadow of doubt that this sensational discovery of mimesis influenced from then on the crystallization of the invisible and paranoiac images which people most of my present paintings with their phantasmal presence. Proud, haughty, ecstatic even over my discovery, I immediately utilized it for purposes of mystification. I proceeded to claim that by virtue of my personal magic I had acquired the ability to animate the inanimate. I would tear a leaf from a mass of these plants, I would substitute my leaf-insect for the leaf by a slight-of-hand and, placing it on the dining room table, I would begin to strike violently all around it with a rounded stone which I presented as the object endowed with magic virtue which was going to bring the leaf to life."

---

* Mimesis: a resemblance which certain living beings assume, either to the environment in which they find themselves, or to the better protected species or to those at whose expense they live.

† The invisible image of Voltaire may be compared in every respect to the mimesis of the leaf-insect rendered invisible by the resemblance and the confusion established between Figure and Background.

"At the beginning of my performance everyone thought the little leaf moved solely because of the agitation which I created around it. But then I would begin to diminish the intensity of my blows until I reduced them to such feeble taps that they could no longer account for the movements of the little leaf-insect which were already clearly independent and differentiated."

"At this moment I completely stopped knocking the table and people then uttered a cry of admiration and general stupefaction upon seeing the leaf really walk. I kept repeating my experiment, especially before fishermen. Everyone was familiar with the plant in question, but no one had ever noticed the phenomenon discovered by me, in spite of the fact that this kind of leaf-insect is to be found in profusion on the plant. When, much later, at the outbreak of the war of 1914, I saw the first camouflaged ships cross the horizon of Cadaques, I jotted down in my notebook of personal impressions and reminiscences something like the following—'Today I found the explanation of my "morros de con*," [for this was what I called my leaf-insect] when I saw a melancholy convoy of camouflaged ships pass by. Against what was my insect protecting himself in adopting this camouflage, this disguise?"

"Disguise was one of my strongest passions as a child."

* This name in Catalonian has a highly pornographic meaning, impossible to translate. It designates a part of the female pudenda and is used by fishermen and peasants to refer to someone or something prodigiously cunning and sly.

KANGAROO

I do not specifically recall Dali ever trying to paint a kangaroo even though he was preoccupied with marsupials in the early 1940's. He did, however, make one amusing reference to it in his speech before the French Academy when he was elected into this august body on May 9, 1979 in Paris.

The artist said that it was an excellent thing the way the continental drift turned out, with Perpignan remaining the center of our (i.e., Dali's) universe, and with Australia drifting far off to the east. This was fortunate for Europe he said, because had Australia not floated off, Spain and France would today be inundated with Kangaroos which would have been the most horrible thing in the world.

His address made a great hit because nobody in the erudite audience understood it. And unfortunately no tape recording of it was made. I recall a later conversation about this topic with Dali. I commented something about how amusing it would have been to see Northern Spain and Southern France "ass deep in kangaroos". We had quite a time with the "ass deep" idiom because he could not see how donkeys fitted in. I had quite a time getting him to grasp the colloquial word "ass" as we use it. He knew what *baisez le cul* meant but could not adjust to our American expression of "kiss my ass".

I recall I once asked Dali if he knew what our English word "fuck" meant. He said he learned out in Carmel where they wintered in the 1940's. People would repeatedly ask him how he liked Carmel and its daily fog that crept in from the sea. He would reply, "Ah-myself is like-ee very much Carmel. Is every morning le sunshine et is possible myself verk very hard in le studio. Et after le luncheon is arriving le fock (fog) et eez divine. Is remain in le room parceque is make fock, fock, fock all afternoon!" His hearers would always laugh uproariously, and people were always coming up to him to ask how he liked Pebble Beach. Then they would roar with laughter when he told them. Finally someone wised him up on fog and fock, and what the latter meant in English. "Eez how myself is learning le word in English many years ah-go."

Over the years Dali's English gradually improved. In business negotiations he never missed a thing. When conversations began to drag, his English declined proportionately, and he lapsed into French, Spanish, and sometimes even Catalan when he was really bored.

LAMB

(See Sheep)

Dali's great miniature of Gala with lamb chops on her shoulder is a comestible matter and indirectly an animal topic. Dali loved both lamb and Gala so he saw no incongruity in this tiny painting on view in the Teatro Museo Dali in Figueres, Spain. His reasoning was cannibalistic: If he could eat one he could eat the other. So lamb is a logical Dalinian category. This little gem of a painting ranks close to *The Specter of Sex-Appeal* among the artist's miniature oils.

In early 1991, a man from California telephoned me to ask if I would endorse a recreation of the original Dali Surrealist Ball in Carmel. He outlined the scenario which I found most un-Dalinian. It was to be a profit making venture and I declined to get involved. Who would have Gala's role? And would she appear in bed with a lion? In 1940 it was a shocker. Today to stage it for money, well it seemed soup already soured, warmed over! So far no one can outdo Dali, and without Dali, there can be no recapturing of the first fine careless rapture of Surrealism's brief flowering in America.

As far as lions are concerned, Dali used to say that when Gala became angry she would roar like the MGM lion!

LIONS

As the train wound slowly around the bay into Oakland, Dali regaled us with reminiscences of the fabulous party he threw at the Del Monte Lodge in Carmel, near Monterey in the early 1940's. (The building is now a Navy School.) The San Francisco Zoo was very cooperative and sent down a lion and several other animals, all of which appeared with Gala in a vast bed. Celebrities came from all over to attend Dali's Surrealist Ball. It was **THE** social event of the West Coast with society people clamoring for invitations. After it was over, Dali said, he was besieged with lucrative offers from other hotels to mastermind a super-party for them. In fact, he went on, if his art failed, he felt he could have made himself quite a career just working professionally to stage spectacular balls at various hotels.

Next to certain creatures (ants and horses), the lion looms large as a detail in many of the artist's works. Dali had many opportunities to see lions in the Barcelona Zoo as a child. In analyzing the painter's evolution, it is impossible to comprehend the seeming complexity of his mind without one's self actually visiting and seeing such things and places as he saw early on in his life in Barcelona. This includes Parque Guell, the Palace of Catalonian Music, the Ramblas and Barcelona's museums new and old; not forgetting the zoo where elephants, rhinoceros and both lions and tigers were found. Remember too, Gaudi's early fountain and La Sagrada Familia, the latter now is making great progress toward completion despite those who hate it and say no such tribute should be made to an architect of another era. (Even Gaudi's sculptures are under attack as being "too modern" of all things!)

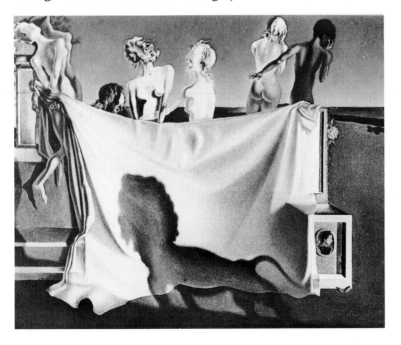

On the several visits we made with Dali to the Barcelona Zoo, I recall how closely he studied the various animals. It was obvious he was there for a purpose, and we dutifully followed the master, chattering with Gala, and leaving him alone while he observed the lions especially.

In all events, the circus **DID** come to Figueres and Dali as a child **DID** see lions both in reality and in books. These indelible impressions are often associated with his formidable father. One is forced to presume this as they are seen over and over in Dali's art. And I recall the artist once remarking that when really angry, his father would "roar like one lion."

The artist felt strongly that he had revealed enough about his family in the *Secret Life*. Thus it was always difficult to pry anything from him about his father, mother, aunt or sister. Gala, if present, would always see that the conversation stayed strictly away from their private and personal lives and especially away from Dali's family and from Paul Eluard, her own first husband.

That his father was a domineering factor in his life even after 1929 there can be no doubt. And I recall Gala in 1956 telling of how she waited in the car while Dali went to the family home on Playa el Laner to see his father who was proud indeed that his estranged son should appear in a Cadillac in Cadaques. Were one to suggest that the lion was a father symbol today, I am sure he would have said, "Myself is no theenk of it, mais is one good idea (a-dee-ha)."

That Dali's relation with his father was a very personal one is substantiated by Ana Maria saying that often when

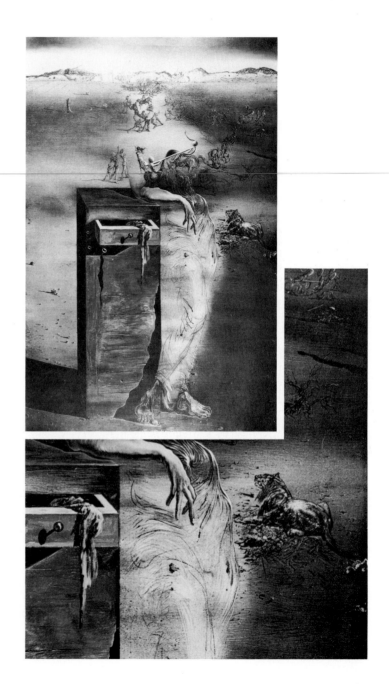

162

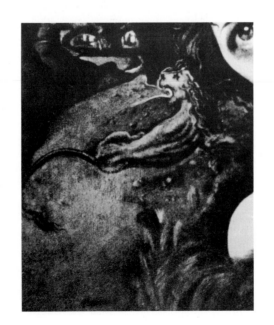

163

Dali would call on his father in Cadaques, Ana Maria could remember seeing Gala walking back and forth down the street some distance away, but never going near the family home herself.

As to identify Dali's depictions of the lion with his imposing father, I feel that this should be left to art critics, the art experts and others who never knew Dali personally nor talked with his father's friends as we did. Few indeed are those now still alive who recall the really rather ferocious notary who could bodily eject a noxious client from his office.

For those who lean to the identity of Dali's father with the artist's lion renderings, there is appended an oil painting Dali did of his father, a formidable personality. But lionesque? I doubt if even Freud would go as far as to make an analogy here. So why the lion symbols? I am sure Dali would have answered, "Parceque myself is like-ee very much le leon!" and nothing more!

In retrospect, it must also be recorded that Dali was never interested in his earlier works. No matter when or where, he would not discuss them in favor of his current schemes and ideas. I well remember on February 6, 1952 when I timorously brought out some reproductions of Dali's early works. We were on the train inching our way to Cedar Falls, Iowa where Dali was to deliver a memorable speech predicting the discovery of the DNA molecule. As the sun set in a winter sky, I did my best to get the artist to comment on his works of the 1920's. He said he approved of the research, but that it was up to me to do the documentation. As to his family, it was impossible to draw

him out. Inevitably the conversation would turn to Gala and his new ideas. Thus to attribute any leonine characteristics to Dali's father, or say the symbol related to the respected local notary is purely one's own interpretations of the often repeated symbol.

The lion appears in many forms, some stylized, some ultra realistic. Often only the shadow of the lion is seen. Sometimes as in *Spain* the female of the species is used. Often the travesty of a lion's head is opposed to a characterized human visage. The grotesque lion of *Vertigo* with popping eyes is a totally anomalous figure adding to the terror of this great 1930 oil.

In a Vogue cover of surrealist furniture a lion's head with dog-like fangs appears and adds an aura of extraneous but absolutely essential atmosphere to an effort that would have been limpid and trite without it.

The challenge of the Dali lion thus is **NOT** to put our own interpretations on it, but to understand why Dali used the symbol where and when he did. So always accept amateur and even professional attributions of Dali's symbols as most probably being wrong, and reflecting only the viewer's ideas, not Dali's. Memories of a child at a circus, or at the zoo in Barcelona? Could be! And nothing more unless the symbol reflects his own personal terror of the animal, for Dali physically was not a very brave person as the start of his eventual decline around 1976 revealed. I was already well aware of the timidity that underlay his seeming insufferable bravado. Thus Dali could very well have been exorcizing his fear of lions by painting them, just as he did with grasshoppers.

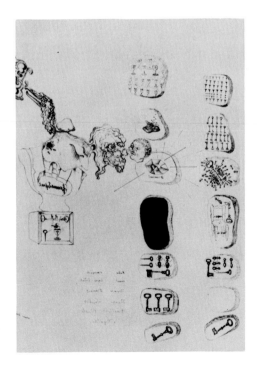

One of Dali's "scandals" which never came off pertained to the royal lion of Venice, the sacred emblem of the city. Dali was staging a ballet there, and to get attention he conceived the idea of painting an image of the city's symbol.

I watched the animal emerge. It was done mainly in red paint on a white pre-prepared canvas. I felt it was a little rough, a little too abstract and splashy and told Dali he should work it over a little more so people would be more likely to recognize it for what it was. He paid no attention to me and said it was done. Then he told us to be on top of the building across from Teatro Fenice at a certain hour.

When we arrived there, we could see Dali across the street on the upper balcony of the theater. The lion picture was brought out and shown to the public below who cheered it. Then the painter took the canvas and placed it on the top of a cage full of pigeons so as to replace the wire lid of the cage.

Then they brought the picture and cage cover and the cage full of pigeons out for the people to see again. This time the cage was placed on the balcony floor and Dali jumped on the canvas, tearing and defacing it, as well as profaning the sacred lion of Venice.

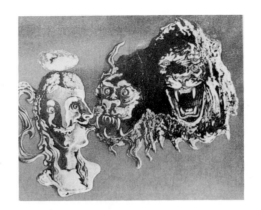

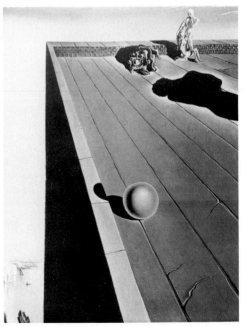

The pigeons flew up and away in a noisy exit, and the minions held up the ruined canvas for all to see. There was absolutely no response from anyone! And there stood the artist, chagrined that no riot had started over the tromping on the image of Venice's sacred lion!

In the postmortem that evening at dinner, we discussed the failure of the "scandal" to inflame the Venetians to a riot. Dali said he hoped for at least a riot as big as the one in Paris when *L'Age d'Or* was shown. The ladies (Eleanor and Gala), however, were not very impressed with the event, although Eleanor and I did chuckle over Dali's stomping on the canvas to free the pigeons. It was not easy to tear, and as we watched him trying to "profane" the lion image, we could not be sure whether to laugh or cry.

LOBSTER

Living on the Mediterranean Sea, Dali learned to love lobsters. The anomaly is that in his art he always depicted lobsters with claws (Maine or North Sea Lobsters) which are quite different from what we call Florida or Mediterranean Lobsters which do not have claws or pincers. The cold water lobsters—red from being cooked—is thus the artist's main depiction both in painting and in his many uses made of lobsters over the years when he was actively image building and myth making with wildly extraneous factors. The aphrodisiacal lobster telephone was thus a sort of surrealist offshoot of Lord Chamberlain's attempt to conciliate Germany and England's difficulties over the telephone. It was also concurrent with Eden's Umbrella seen in certain works of the late 1930's.

Gala and the Angelus of Millet Immediately Preceding the Arrival of the Conic Anamorphoses—*1933*

Dali went through a sort of fetish crises toward the end of his formal surrealist years involving lobsters in various ways. In the 1930's he used lobsters in a dress design for Schiaparelli, and shortly thereafter he undertook his *Dream of Venus* Exhibit for the New York 1939 World's Fair. The studies for this elaborate 1939 Fair Exhibit involved many nude models against whom he was juxtaposing lobsters. Fortunately the girl playing the piano underwater and the other swimmers did not have to face the live animals in the tank. In Dali's bestiary, lobsters, especially when placed on a poor model's pudenda, remain a sort of test of his perversity with their significance in the main being gustatory and something that did not become prominent in his act until after he came to America. I say this despite the cooked lobster's appearance on the man's head in the 1933 panel *Gala and the Angelus of Millet Immediately Preceding the Arrival of the Conic Anamorphoses.* This was one of his earliest depictions of the lobster in his serious works. Many photographs exist of him with various nude models with lobsters

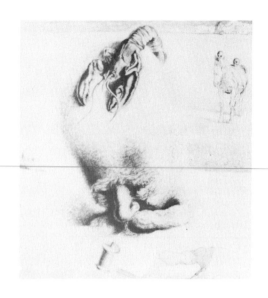

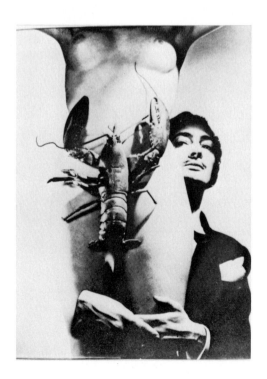

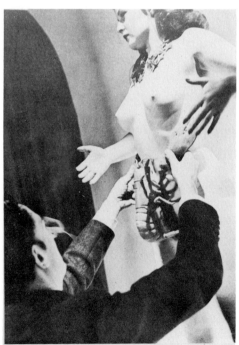

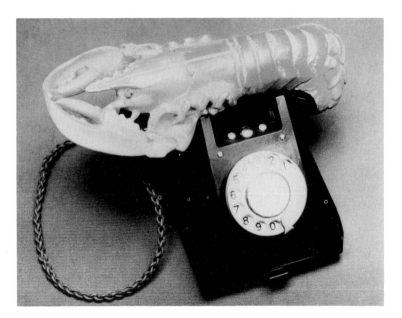

resting on their bodies, and in the pubic area. The symbolism was never explained by the artist. The incongruity, however, was an attention getter, and that after all, was an essential part of Dali's post surrealist image creating years.

Attempts to rationalize Dali's fascination with the lobster or his succession of the other fetishes over the years always seem to result in misinterpretations of Dali's surrealistic forays. Indeed one purpose of *Animal Crackers* is to sharpen up our focus on just one aspect of the artist's total genius. Attempts to read meanings into Dali's zoo or his intense preoccupations with the various elements of his bestiary, however, are beyond the scope of these representations and what they reveal about his unique mind and superb draftsmanship. Thus as to lobsters: Dali loved to eat them! But what other contemporary artist could paint or draw one as superbly as Dali? Or could it have been a Pop Art manifestation years before its time?

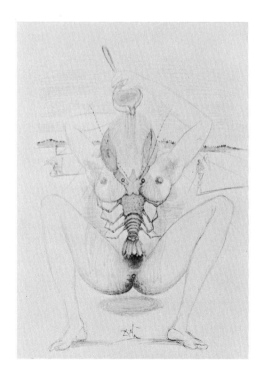

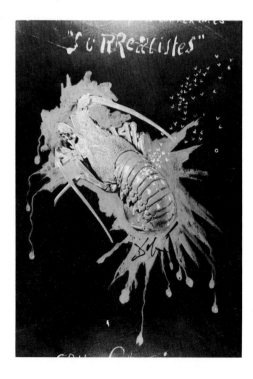

MAGGOTS

(See Worms, Porcupine, and Hedgehog)

On page 94 of Dali's *Secret Life* of 1943, he graphically illustrates maggots eating his pet hedgehog Q.V. Dali makes several references to the colors of decaying corpses which he likened to jewels.

MINOTAURE

Dali's cover for *Minotaure Magazine,* No. 8, 1936, is a landmark item in his bestiary for one main reason. Picasso was very heavy into minotaures, and Dali created his own distinctive version complete with lobster genitals, a drawer in the chest—and in the upper right a truly prophetic illustration of the cloud to be given off by the atom bomb some years in the future. (The eclectic theme is actually shown four times).

In my book *Dali-Picasso, Picasso-Dali* for the first time ever, I pointed out the differences and similarities of the two Spanish heroes of modern painting. That Dali could be heroically creative when up against his older contemporary is exemplified in his Minotaure cover for this distinguished but short-lived periodical.

Parenthetically it should be observed that a minotaure as killed by Theseus in the labyrinth built by Daedalus, can have the head of a bull on a man's torso, or a bull's body with the head of a man.

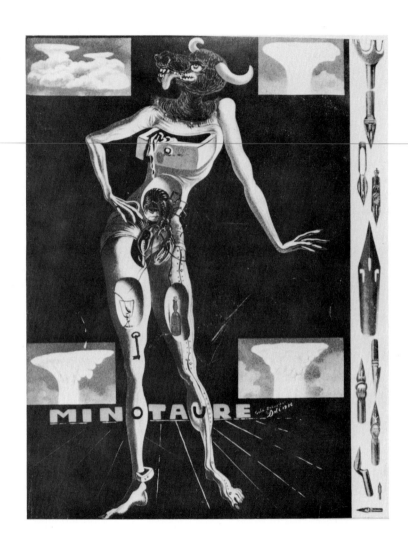

Dali *— 1936*   **Picasso** *— 1933*

Picasso pictured himself as a minotaure over and over, often with a nude lady. Dali, on the other hand, did not follow his contemporary's obsession and purposely let Picasso dominate this particular theme source.

The main difference to note here is that Picasso was actually a beast-monster as has now been seen in his treatment of his many women. Dali, on the other hand, was always faithful to Gala and was more of an esoteric and less bull-like personality. Picasso's productivity was also many, many times greater than that of his countryman. Dali watched Picasso like a hawk, but he never made the fatal error of trying to outproduce him. So far their similarities and differences have only been evaluated by myself. The art establishment's mores do not permit the mention of the two Spaniards in the same breath, yet no more fascinating study in the evolution of ideas could be made as their two minotaures prove.

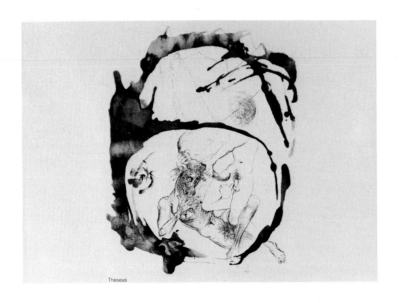

Theseus

MONSTERS

This classification is necessarily a broad one both because of the scope of Dali's imagination and the various meanings attached to the word itself. These range from abnormalities and part animal, part human creatures on to the unicorn, and the out of the ordinary or unexpected.

In my analysis of Dali's paranoiac-critical creative method of generating new ideas, it is pointed out that Dali's images were eidetically perceived in his brain complete with color, but in many cases without any verbalization being involved. This meant there are often no labels (i.e., words) existing which can describe his depictions.

Thus the term "monster" with all its various meanings is really apt in many instances because it is virtually impossible to describe the subject any other way than in the latitude usage as built into this word. Thus these Dalinian "monsters" are limited to a relatively few examples precisely because so many of his beasts are monstrous in many eyes.

Under Frog [Q.V.] you will find another example of a Dali monster. Here his interpretation of a creature in (*The Maze*) a Sandoz story is significant because it can also be viewed upside down where a face emerges from the figure of the frog monster.

  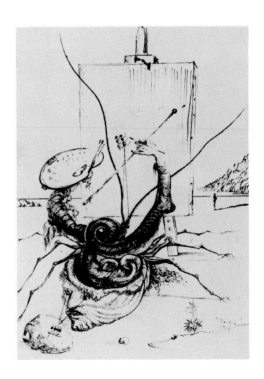

MOTH

We also asked Dali about the moth shot in *Un Chien Andalou*. Here there is a moth which is gradually approached by the camera to reveal a death's head in the natural coloring of the moth. Dali said that this was 100% his own idea, and that the name of the species referred to the death's head it carries on its back. I asked him what he thought of Luis Buñuel. He said, "Only little echoes of Dali's ideas is remine. Is no much af-ter Dali." I said he was wrong, and that Buñuel had done some really superb Surrealist things such as the Last Supper scene in *Viridiana*. Dali listened with no comment. I asked if he would ever collaborate with Buñuel again. "Nevaire," he replied. I persisted, "But Dali, should two people who changed the whole course of movie history deny the world such a joint effort?" Again, he said nothing, but left me with a brown look, firm but not sad.

The pursuit of Dali's Death's Head Moth has occupied many years. It comes from Madagascar and is called the Urania or "Sunset" moth. I finally was able, through the Butterfly People of San Juan, to obtain an example of the moth for the Dali archives. To me it is a supreme example of Dali's ability to combine his erudition with his ability to present us with the unusual. Seen in the film, *Un Chien Andalou*, the emergence of the death's head suddenly darkens the whole mood of the movie script. It is a perfect example of the rare chemistry that made movie history by uniting the diverse and extraordinary talents of Dali and Luis Buñuel.

The Death's Head Moth vies in impact with the scorpions which battle in *L'Age d'or*. These unfamiliar insects were found in no other films of the era or in succeeding years.

While Dali's collaboration with Buñuel was relatively brief after their school years in Madrid, still the two films that evolved remain movie landmarks, and in both films animals such as the cow, the pig, the decaying donkeys, and the ants play significant parts.

OCELOTS

After this adventure the artist said, "OK. Pour aujourdhui is suffi." But Elly said, "Ocelots. You own two." "Oh, les ocelots. Myself is own one. Is no very interesting only for le small manifestation. Is very good for throwing in le swimming pool."

If there were any real hegemony in Dali's zoo it could conceivably begin with Dali's ocelots, first one, then two. The stylish but slinky animals appearing early in the 1960's are associated as much with the Irish adventurer Peter Moore as they are with Dali and Gala.

By the time Moore turned up and took over the drudgery of Dali's menage which Gala had always taken care of, the painter was phasing out his image building antics such as the arquebus and bulletism. The ocelots filled the gap to a conservative degree, there being first one and then two, both of which were housed in Moore's room not that of the artist.

The St. Regis, of course, frowned on animals, but Dali's hotel bill was sufficiently large (along with the business he drew to the hotels which were his headquarters during his winter hunting season) that the management was willing to overlook the occasional pee pee of the ocelots as they cowered and tugged at their leashes among the forest of feet in the hotel lobby.

Our last impression of these nuisance animals was in Spain. There Moore's gracious wife invited us to lunch along with Marc Lacroix, an experimentalist photographer, and his wife. We were in the roof garden on top of Moore's house there overlooking the Bay of Cadaques and across from the flat Marcel Duchamp always occupied. Moore picked up one of the ocelots and vigorously French-kissed it, despite the animal's squirmy distaste for the gesture. This slobbering with the cat tongue to tongue revolted both the Lacroix' and ourselves. Finally the animal broke loose from Moore's embrace and fled across the red tile roof tops—and that was the last we ever saw of the poor unlamented pet.

Dali and the ocelot added to the confusion of unpacking our entire collection for the Dali show in Huntington Hartford's Gallery of Modern Art in New York December 20, 1965.

Moore's soul kissing one of the ocelots is not a spectacle which either ourselves or the Lacroix' could ever possibly forget—nor would undoubtedly the animal. We felt that exchanging spit with the beast went well beyond the pale.

Our memories of the ocelots in the Meurice in Paris, in the Palace Hotel in Madrid and the Ritz in Barcelona are part of a frenetic era in Dali's career. Our personal feeling was that at this point he should not have kept the ocelots in such surroundings, and that Moore as the animal keeper should have not catered to having the poor creatures around. Needless to say we and many others were greatly relieved when both Moore and the ocelots were eliminated from Dali's bustling entourage.

On one occasion we were with Dali and Gala in the garden back of their house with its phallic-shaped swimming pool, when Dali suddenly reached down and picked up one of the ocelots and threw it into the pool. The animal swam bravely to shore, scrambled out, shook itself and slunk off to lick itself dry.

Eleanor was shocked and said Dali was cruel. He laughed and replied, "On le contrary, le ocelot is like-ee very much le water! Et besides, le an-i-mal is no good for anything save for throwing in le pool!

The crack in the floor of Dali's studio requires some elaboration. As the size of Dali's paintings grew, with *The Madonna of Port Lligat* of 1948-49, the artist had a long slot cut in the floor next to the south wall of his second floor studio. A pulley arrangement allowed canvases too big for his easel to be lowered into the slot so he could always work at eye level. (Later it was motorized, "quand is arriving le monay.") This slot opened over a storage room below where fishermen stored their nets and traps, and which was always locked. One could however, where the ground floor door open, sometime see the lower portion of the canvas Dali was working on, incongruously hanging over tarry nets, and other of the fishermen's paraphernalia.

OCTOPUS

"**A**h, yes. Le octopus. Alzo is make one vatercolor of le octopus. Is create one head of Beethoven. Is remine in le studio quand y yam leave for Paris. Et alzo is make le lithograph avec le octopus, et one draw-ving for Lucas.

"One udder time in Port Lligat myself is now remember, is having two life octopus in le studio. In one moment is fall one brush in one crack in le floor, mais is very far et is no possible recuperate le brush que is my favorite. So is attach one string of le octopus et is lower le animal through le hole in le floor et le arm of le octopus is grasp le brush et is pull up so, et recover le brush. Is very easy et proof qu y yam one genius (jay-nee-ous)."

Dali's fascination with the octopus extended far beyond eating it in favorite Catalan dishes. He often visualized it as typifying a head of Medusa. In several occasions he pressed one of the animals on paper to horrify those of us unable to juxtapose the octopus idea and human flesh. A lithograph—a rare one made by this technique actually was sold by Woolworth's in the primal heyday of Dali's genuine "lithographs." It was a sellout.

Even in the masterworks there is a small section made by pressing an octopus onto a wet underpainting, and then of course working the result into the adjacent surfaces. It is a constant reminder of the artist's closeness to the Mediterranean and all its creatures.

Dali often would greet his fisherman friends on the stone wharf in front of his house and look over their hauls, while Katarina was on hand to get the fish for the Dali's dinner. Few artists, as I have said, ever lived closer to nature than our Spanish (Catalan) friend who missed no details of the harvest as many of the fish in his early works prove so well. [I tried octopus in its ink in Madrid, and found; a) it was rather too tough and rubbery b) one was enough. Small crisp octopus is a little more tasty.]

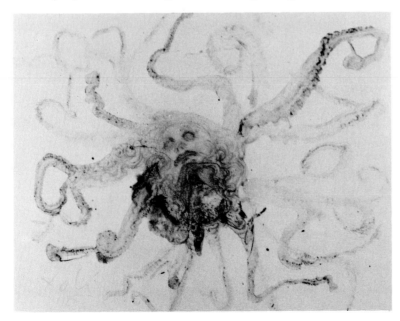

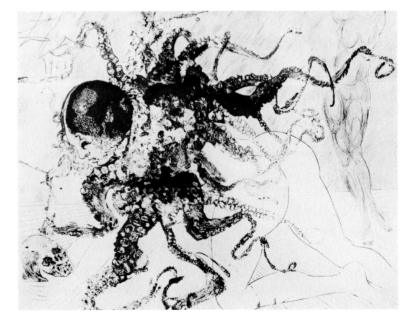

OYSTERS

"In July, neither woman nor oysters." Salvador Dali, *Diary of a Genius,* Doubleday, 1956, Page 29—entry for July 1st 1952.

I recall discussing the master's dictum, and told him that the Spanish seem to have gone us one better, because we are not supposed to eat oysters in July. I said to Dali that our folklore limited eating oysters to all months containing the letter "R", and that in months without R oysters could not be safely consumed in America.

The net result was that I could not discover why in Spain women were so related to oysters. As I remember the talk, I got the feeling that it was distinctly impolitic for a courtier to dare match a proverb or a folkloric matter with his king!

Eleanor's favorite story relates to Dali's oysters. He told us of a waiter in a hotel on the Mediterranean. The man had somehow damaged a hotel painting and was about to be discharged. The waiter came to Dali and asked him to help save his job by repairing the painting. This the artist did.

At this time, it was found that the local oyster beds were contaminated, and it was recommended they not be eaten. The waiter knew Dali loved oysters and brought him a dozen in gratitude for his repairing of the painting. He put them before the artist and waited obsequiously around while Dali with a great deal of hesitation ate all the oysters. He could not hide them in a planter or avoid eating them in any way, he said, so there was no option for him but to eat them or offend the poor grateful waiter.

The oysters made Dali quite ill during the night and he said the episode taught him a fundamental lesson. That is, NEVER be nice to anyone, or you will regret it! I can still see Dali as he related the tale in the Hotel in Cannes in the gold ornate dining room in the spring of 1974 when we were en route to Spain with the Dalis.

PARROT

The parrot is seen in a rare watercolor once the property of Edward F. W. James, Dali's mentor during the 1930's. The artist was well aware that parrot feathers were used during the 1920's when color photography was being developed. The reason was that light was uniformly reflected from them which was constant and invariable in its properties and wave-lengths.

The birds seen in *The First Days of Spring* 1929, also are present for the same reason, and to commemorate the appearance of early colored photographs.

A later watercolor of a parrot by Dali has been published as a reproduction in Paris by Robert Descharnes, demonstrating Dalinian Continuity.

PEACOCK

The peacock is the subject of a Dali graphic issued by the publisher Pierre Argillet. It depicts the eyes of the expanded tail of the bird. The artist once gave us a rare gift. It is a print of the graphic work, hand-colored by himself. Gala was very resentful over her husband's generosity and scolded him mercilessly for being so nice to us. The same design was also enlarged and made into a tapestry which is quite spectacular.

PIG

(BOAR)

"**P**igs," I said. "Did you ever have an experience with pigs?" Dali lightened up at once. "Ah, yes. Le Pig. In the Muli de la Torre, Sr. Pitchot is keep many pigs, perhaps twelve. Is very clean. Is le floor of...(marble — as he tapped the marble topped cocktail table with his cane to signify the sort of stone floor used in the pig barn.) Is always wash. Et one day is arrive Dali in le barn et is approach one wvoman's (female) peeg. Is very large dees wvoman's pig. Myself is climb on le back of le giant pig pour catch one ride. Is walk a leetle, mais su-dent-ly is becoming very wild. Myself is falling off on le floor et is nearly kill-ed. Everybody is afraid que y yam almost dead."

Neither Eleanor nor I ever recall Dali eating pork. His main diet was fish. He loved lamb chops, and both he and Gala would eat a small filet or chicken. Crisp bacon, however, was one of his breakfast items.

There is in Spain a very gamey sort of ham which is tough, leathery and from a sort of wild pig which is very popular and which Dali would sometimes partake. Actually it is from a wild boar, if I recall, a jabali and not from the domesticated animal.

The most conspicuous pig in Dali's animal kingdom is the one whose eye appears in the shocking opening scene of *Un Chien Andalou*. Here a close-up, ostensibly of a human eye, where first a long cloud crosses the moon, and then a razor is seen ostensibly slicing open a human eye in one of the artist's most shocking efforts: a grim bit of surrealism indeed, and one viewers never forget.

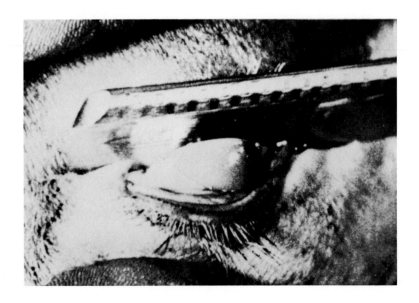

Excerpt from Dali's Private Dictionary

The pig is the one that never retreats and opens the way among the impurities of consumer society and advances gluttonously.

I am a pig that goes toward the "non plus ultra". That's me. But eliminating the "non" and leaving the "plus ultra", because the pigs never retreat; jesuitically they go from side to side through thousands of innumerable viscosities, but always a step further ahead.

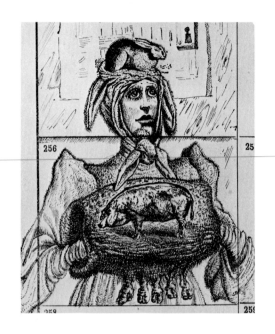

PIGEONS

Life in Port Lligat was fairly rigorous. Snobbish and elite visitors were always a little taken aback with the stark simplicity of Dali's life for eight to nine months of the year. His pigeon loft was for real and the birds were part of his diet. Fish were, however, by far the main portion of his regimen—fish from the sea in front of the Bay of Port Lligat.

Dali's use of pigeons is seen in one of his illustrations for *Benvenuto Cellini's Autobiography* made in 1945. His career as an illustrator was a distinguished one and countless animals appear, often extraneously, to add a special Dalinian touch to the book in question. He was truly a hard working man after the war started and the couple took refuge in New York.

A new edition of his work as an illustrator is in process and it will, hopefully, further reveal many more examples of Dali's treatment of his bestiary. The exciting thing about Dali's illustrations are that they are never trite and appeared in an era—a decade of war. There the concept of illustrated books was at an all time low.

189

PORCUPINE

(See Hedgehog, Maggots and Worms)

On page 15 of *The Unspeakable Confessions of Salvador Dali* the painter mentions a rather grisly experience with a pet animal. The details of this revelation of the decaying beast are very close to those related in his *Secret Life* on page 94 where he illustrates the dead animal. In the text that follows the beast is called a porcupine.

Chevalier's superior translation of the earlier reference and use of the word "hedgehog" is clearly the animal involved and **NOT** a porcupine as given in the "*Confessions.*" There are many examples of inept translation in the latter book, so one is justified in assuming that even though Dali was "crazy," he would not have had a porcupine for a pet. The story as given in the Confessions on page 15 follows:

As a child, I also had a porcupine that disappeared one day. A week later, I found it dead in the henhouse. But I remember that at first I thought it was alive, for its bristles were being so actively moved by the packet of maggots oozing around the corpse. The head was disappearing under a greenish gelatinous mess. At that moment I lived to its delirious limit the strange fascination of that death, that unspeakable corpse, the rotting stink that rose from the biological offal. I was able to tear my eyes away only because my legs were buckling under me and I had to flee the stench. It was just the time when the gathering of lime-blossoms started, and as I came out of the henhouse, a-tremble with horror, I was blessed with the soothing scent of their aromatic leaves. But the fascination was too great. I held my breath and went back into the chicken coop once more to inspect the decomposing carrion. Then, back out to breathe the fresh air, and back again into the henhouse.

191

Stench, fragrance, shadow and light, corpse and beauty of flowers: they kept alternating in a hysterical ballet until I was totally overcome by the desire, the need to touch that pile of vermin. I resisted at first and, the better to outwit my horrible desire, tried to jump over the porcupine. But by some sort of need to fail, I slipped and fell, with my nose almost right down in the mess of worms. I was horribly disgusted and, grabbing a grubbing-hoe, which to me was endowed with fetishistic powers, used the flat of the blade slowly to crush the porcupine: its skin finally gave way, revealing the teeming flesh beneath. I dropped the hoe and started to run away. I was breathless; the shock was overwhelming. I felt crushed. Yet I came back to retrieve my soiled fetish, which I then went and soaked endlessly in the waters of a stream, before throwing it down on the stacks of lime-blossoms drying in the sun. But I still had to let it soak in the dew of daybreak before it lost the stench of putrefaction. I had just brushed up against the horror of death.

The porcupine is described as any one of a number of related gnawing animals, specifically (a) the old world porcupine bearing long stiff erectile spines sometimes a foot in length and easily detached from the body. In my experience the spines are barbed.

The hedgehog by contrast is an insectivorous quadruped with a shaggy coat and sharp spines on the back which bristle and form a hedge-like defense when the animal curls up.

Thus the porcupine is totally different from the hedgehog, and I stand by my opinion that the foregoing quotation incorrectly refers to a porcupine when it should have said hedgehog.

PORTERIA

(Oreille de Santa Lucia)

Dali next pulled King Farouk's snuff box from his pocket and took out the porteria, which he always carried for good luck. I asked why the little shell "foot" of the snail was not orange like so many we have seen. "Some is orange, mais no all." he said. He told us that the shellfish's "door" is very important for three reasons. First, it has the aspect of an ear, and the ear has always been very important in his works, such as the large ear and the virgin painted with dots and bought by Mrs. Heinz, the Pope's ear concept and so on.

Second, if you put the porteria in vinegar, the acid attacks the calcium carbonate in it. Since this was deposited in spiral form, the result is that the little-button like piece of shell spins as the CO_2 gas comes off of it as acid attacks the shell. This phenomenon always delighted the children, and he has never forgotten it.

And finally, he told us that the porteria represented a door to shut out the world. When the shellfish drew it closed, it prepared for hibernation. Thus it reduced its metabolic rate and extended its survival rate in a hostile environment because it was protected by the "porteria," or foot. Then he went on to add that the porteria was significant in his cosmogony for another reason too. One side of it is wrinkled, and the other is smooth. It contains thirty-seven wrinkles, he said, "Exactly like le anus of le human," there was thus a metaphysical connection here which he felt was very important in his view of natural philosophy. He placed the little object carefully back in King Farouk's box, showing us how he could change the F which was separated from the rest of the name to a D in the raised lettering on the cover, then returned thrusting it deeply into his pocket.

These doors or feet are the small button which some snails have, that when pulled into place by the animal render it totally impenetrable by an enemy. (My notes spell the name for this button-like "shell" Portoleria.)

Both Arturo Camanada, Ramon Salart and Dali gave us samples of this door or foot. Some of them were orange, some yellow or white tinted with those colors. They are highly regarded little keepsakes in Cadaques and I still treasure two or three of them for sentimental reasons. My journal extract covers about all I know of porteria or Oreille [ear] of Santa Lucia. To Dali it was clearly a good luck symbol which he carried like his little piece of dry wood for which we once had to make a search of his hotel room in Arcachon on one of our travels with them. Gala told us of another time he felt he had lost his good luck talismen and the hectic search she made for them, even down to the laundry of the St. Regis before it was eventually found. Dali would often take one or the other talismen out and rub it when negotiations or some crucial meeting or sale was pending. The artist was definitely superstitious, and I was always careful never to belittle his belief in his good luck symbols or fetishes. This went all the way to his gingerly touching dog droppings with the toe of his shoe for good luck.

RABBIT

A rare animal story is recounted in a book by L. S. Klepp. The author elaborates rather too freely on his rabbit story. The Dali's did keep a dove cote and often ate pigeons. They also did have rabbits at one point.

It is true that Gala was fond of one which Arturo did prepare for their dinner one time. I recall Gala telling us of the incident. It remains, however, quite apocryphal in Mr. Klepp's version because the Dalis had both a cook (Katrina) and a maid, and Gala would not be caught dead cooking anything.

Arturo was always there, and took care of the whole establishment so it was highly questionable that they debated about the future of the rabbit. His version of the incident, however, is worth noting here because it is a rare reference to the private lives of this couple who lived in one of the most isolated and remote spots ever inhabited by a major artist: that is Port Lligat which in the early days was a real trek.

Natural Affection and Edible Love

When they were already quite old, the famous painter Salvador Dali and his wife, Gala, had a pet rabbit, who lived with them and followed them around everywhere, and of whom they were very fond. Once, they were about to embark on a long trip, and they debated long into the night what to do with the rabbit. It would have been difficult to take him along and equally difficult to entrust him to somebody else, because the rabbit was uneasy with strangers. The next day Gala prepared lunch and Dali enjoyed the excellent food until he realized he was eating rabbit meat. He got up from the table and ran to the bathroom, where he vomited up his beloved pet, the faithful friend of his waning days. Gala, on the other hand, was happy that the one she loved had passed into her guts, caressing them and becoming the body of his mistress. For her there existed no more perfect fulfillment of love than eating the beloved. Compared to this merging of bodies, the sexual act seemed to her no more than ludicrous tickling.

RAM

(see Goat)

Dali portrayed the ram in a 1928 oil which clearly was a reference to the animal as depicted by Max Ernst. The dictionary defines it as a male sheep.

The goat is "a horned ruminant quadruped of the genus Capra. The horns are hollow turned backward, rough and annular on the surface. The male is generally bearded under the chin."

The Ram — *1928*

RAT

Dali's gouache on a photograph shows a sweet young infant holding a decayed rat in his mouth. Called *The Perverse Polymorph of Freud,* this painting was shown at the Hartford Gallery in 1965-1966 and I suspect came to the exhibition from Gala's own vault in the Manhattan storage warehouse where all her treasures were kept. I went there twice with her, one time to rescue *The Ecumenical Council* after we bought it. It was loosely rolled and flung across a pile of her treasures. The painting had been in storage for five years before I summoned up the courage to purchase it. Rest assured, $100,000 in pesetas was a heavy bundle which I helped Gala stuff into her luggage!

The next reference to a rat I can recall is in the Skira story as recorded in my Dali journal and which follows:

"As we slowly wound the last miles, Dali told me how generous Picasso had been to him in the early 1930's, advancing him the money to go to America, and also recommending him to Skira, the publisher, as the best man to illustrate an edition of *Les Chants de Maldoror.* Once the contract was signed and the work underway, the artist said that Mr. Skira became extraordinarily elusive. He told how he waited one day in Skira's office "to catch some money."

Skira saw Dali waiting for him in the hall, and beat a hurried retreat. Dali then curled up on the sofa in the publisher's office to wait Skira out. Hours and hours went by, but, the artist went on, several times he had to "make pee pee." So instead of leaving the office, he peed in Skira's brass umbrella stand. Finally, Skira came back to get some papers, and not seeing Dali on the couch came into the office. Dali sprang up and collared him, and managed to collect a little money for his etchings—an event which he described with a characteristic gesture of folding money into his coat pocket. Some days later, Dali had the satisfaction of hearing Skira tell someone, "You know, a rat or something must have died in my office. It smells simply terrible and I cannot find out what the odor is or where it is coming from. But it is horrible!"

RHINOCEROS

"**E**t le rhinoceros. Is make two prints avec le ani-mal. Et alzo is project one magazine, *Le Rhinoceros* avec Skira, mais is no arrive. Alzo in le *Manifeste Mystique* is appear one drawving of le rhinocerous. Le more important is le corn (horn). Is point in le sky. Is point to heaven. Is le total opposite of le beast que is very fat et 'eavy, et close of le ground. Et le corn is one very good aphrodisiac, mais is all sold-ded in China. Le corn is appear in *Nature Morte Vivante* very real, et in *l'Ascension,* in *le Infanta* in many osser of me verks. Is no possible tell all. You is remember dees et expline." (Corn, of course, is Dalinian for horn.)

One of the earliest manifestations of the artist's rhinocerotic preoccupation was seen in a relatively tiny detail of *Madonna of Port Lligat* on the lower left of the table in the bottom foreground. Innocuously, it foretold a rather disconcerting symbolism but still a truly Dalinian one, disturbing though it was to the critics and ourselves as well. Esthetically and artistically obscure though the rhinoceros period seemed, the improbable symbol was destined to be with us for a decade.

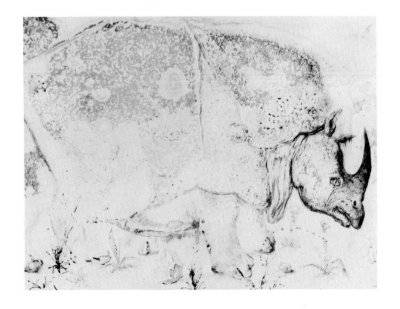

What underlay this fetish? Really it was Dali's discovery that the rhinoceros horn is considered a superb aphrodisiac by the Chinese. Their demand for it was intense and Dali was taken by the impatience with which the Chinese people in Paris awaited the arrival of the annual shipment. The artist did not even flinch when I told him that there was a danger of the rhinoceros becoming extinct to satisfy the Chinese demand for its keratinous (fibrous not bony) horn.

Dali admired Dürer's depiction of a rhinoceros precisely because it was still partly allegorical. His own infatuation with this ungainly animal, and especially its heaven-pointing horn, began when he was well along in his classic era. The 1940's produced a series of varied oils,

beginning with his *Madonna of Port Lligat* and his *Christ of St. John of the Cross*. These stunning masterworks were followed by his *Mystic Manifest* and his vision of Vermeer's *Lacemaker* as capable of being broken down and recreated using rhinoceros horns. To accomplish this the artist got permission to transcribe his rhinocerotic version of the *Lacemaker* in the Louvre. It was a paranoiac-critical bombshell that led to a long obsession with the rhinoceros.

His investigations were intense, and even took him into the rhinoceros pen at the Paris Zoo. His use of the rhinoceros horn was concurrent with his atomic reactions where he began to portray everything he painted as being blown into fragments by modern science and, of course, that included the poor rhinoceros.

One of the masterworks was the 90½ by 56⅔ inch canvas called *Assumpta Corpuscularia Lapislazulina* of 1952. This was accomplished with a real plethora of rhinocerotic symbolism. Our pleas to Dali to ease up on his emphasis on the rhinoceros fell on deaf ears. Nobody could influence the obdurate master, and he would pay no attention to the adverse criticism of the art commentators who could find nothing meritorious in the least in his infatuation with the lumbering beast. As usual Dali was the winner! In 1958 he came up with a canvas that triumphed over everything especially our pleas to give up on the rhinoceros. *Velasquez Painting the Infanta with the Lights and Shadows of His Own Glory* depicted the princess with her head comprised of rhinoceros horns! It was, we felt, perhaps his finest and most Spanish oriented work. It also marked pretty much the end of his rhinocerotic obsession.

Velasquez Painting the Infanta Margarita with the Lights and Shadows of His Own Glory — *1958*

This blending of Velasquez and Dali and his fantasies about rhinoceros horns remains one of his most painterly and masterful canvases. It was certainly an aesthetic triumph and typically Dalinian. And while it did not end his absorption with depicting atomic particles and exploding objects, still it did more or less phase out the little lamented rhinoceros—an animal which only Dali could have possibly tamed and utilized, while further marking himself as one of our greatest creative geniuses!

EXCERPT FROM DALI'S PRIVATE DICTIONARY

I don't like animals or children. I only admire the rhinoceros for his enormous cosmic strength. Not long ago Princess Rethy offered me a white one, of a special race raised in the Congo.

The rhinoceros horn is the logarithmic curve of beauty. I discovered it copying *The Lacemaker* by Vermeer of Delft.

The divine pig that is me — did I forget to say it? — has a rhinoceros horn. To be truthful I am a rhinoceros, but with a mustache.

The ground-up rhinoceros horn is a powerful aphrodisiac. The beauty and Eros are one. This admirable animal is not satisfied carrying a sex on its nose; his mating lasts for about an hour.

Studying the behind of a rhinoceros I discovered that it represents exactly a folded sunflower.

ROACHES

Recent research into Dali's party at Carmel in Pebble Beach where he placed a lion in a bed during one of their various winters there in the 1940's and 1950's, uncovered one of his pranks. The artist caught some roaches and painted eyes on their backs. When the local revelers returned to the Lodge after a bibulous evening, he released the creatures in the lobby. The resulting sensation was never forgotten by those who witnessed the ensuing panic. Dali's legend-making clearly has deep and persistent roots unlike most of his less spectacular and inventive contemporaries whose personalities are today lost behind the veil of their art.

SARDINES

(See Anchovies)

SCARAB

On May 8, 1974, we sat chatting with Dali in the large salon of the Ritz Hotel in Barcelona. Dali recalled once painting an open eye on the back of a scarab beetle. When the scarab crawled around on the table, it was like a magical apparition of a human eye moving mysteriously about on its own location. "Very hypnotic," the artist commented.

Beyond is a Dali drawing of the Scarab with an eye on its back which he made on a copy of a letter from Fleur Cowles, author of an excellent early biography of the master, during the discussion of Dali's animals on the S.S. France, April, 1974. As I recall it, we had some problem with the French and Spanish version of scarab as pronounced by the master. He gave up trying to explain it, and asked me for a piece of paper. I refused to tear a page out of my notebook and handed him Fleur Cowles' letter reproduced here.

(There recently surfaced a story about Dali painting eyes on the backs of roaches when he was in Carmel during the 1940's. This is recounted under roaches Q.V.)

The scarab is described as a "beetle held sacred by the ancient Egyptians. An image of the beetle cut from a stone or gem, often engraved with symbols on the flat underside and formerly worn as a charm."

This could account for Dali's fascination with the eporculum, the door on the snail shell called Porteria (Q.V.) He was a very superstitious man. I have often seen him hide all his change (and mine) around a hotel room as we checked out. for good luck he said, and so if he ever returned there he would have some money!

Now decades later, I still have visions of Dali during our travels asking me for small change as we were leaving various hotel rooms. I would hand him what change I had (or part of it as I wised up to his fetish). Just before he closed the door he would then throw the coins back into the room. At first I protested and he explained that this brought good luck. This was just one of the master's superstitions that rubbed off onto me, only I now leave a single penny being less prodigal than the painter.

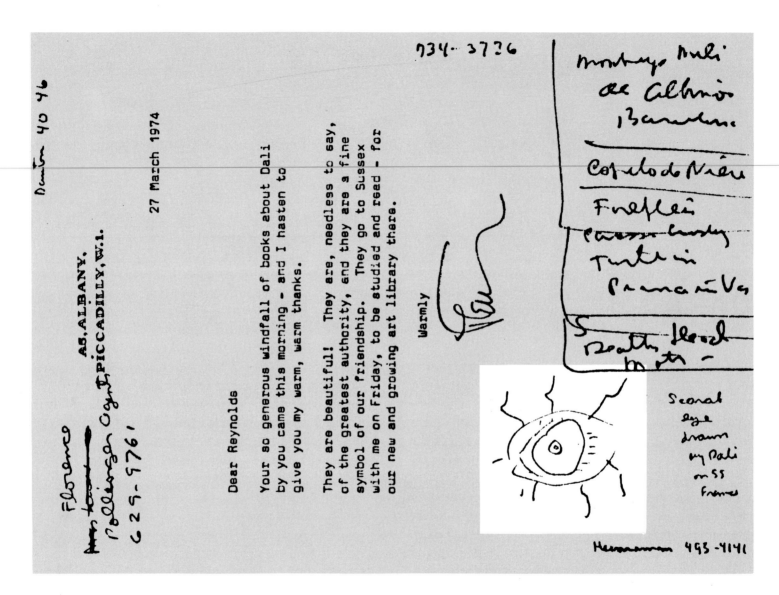

Dali Drawing of Scarab with eye on back made on
copy of letter during discussion of Dali's Animals on the
S.S. France, April, 1974.

SEAGULLS

"Et also is involv-éd stuffed seagulls. Is arrive many for le same painting. Ah, yes. Is arrive in New York le day que y am leave le news que le police is very close of recover le *Tuna Fishing.* Myself is all le time utilize le stuffed animals. Is one swvallo in *Nature Morte Vivant* que is stuffed. Et alzo le swan in le library, et le giraffe, et le horse for Pubol que one man is bring in le Meurice Hotel is stuff-ed. Is much more peaceful quand si is no alive."

"Myself is now remember one sing of le Tuna. Quand myself is paint le seagull in dees pictures, le beerd (bird) is 'ave one life fish in le mout (mouth). Arturo is coming one day et tell is no right. Le gaviotta no hold le fish in dees manner, nevaire, parceque is no possible swallow, et alzo le seagull is always swvallo le fish so le head is coming feerst et apres le tail. So is no swvallo in dees way is possible choking.

So is necessary myself immediately change le gaviotta in le *Tuna Fishing.*"

As the train approached Oakland, Dali went into the lounge car. I joined him there under the domed roof. "Divine," he said pointing up with his cane to the plastic inverted skylight, "Divine like the bowl of the sky in my *Lapis-lazuli!*" Just as he spoke a large seagull flew over and let fly, splat on the dome. "Parfait!" Dali exclaimed in great excitement, "Is create one perfect an-gel. Look les vings! is now even more divine." "Yes," I commented, "the dome is now a complete Meifren" as I pointed to the bird shit splatter. (I was referring to the fact that in Spain Meifren's art which was often done in white and gray and therefore locally referred to degradingly as "pigeon shit art,") "No," Dali sharply retorted. "Is much too green to be Meifren!" Never overlook Dali's knowledge of his Catalan precursors and contemporaries. He opened up a whole new world of painting for us, and we continue to study the Catalan painters whose works, often subtly, clearly influenced his own evolution as a young artist mainly prior to 1929.

Sea Urchin

"Et no forget le draw-ving avec le sea urchin. Le draw-ving is make of le urchin avec le ink on le e-speen. Is love la e-speen (spine). Is make one injection of adrenalin pour create le movement of les e-spines."

This is a reference to one of Dali's experiments in action painting. There was the bomb set off to blast nails into a copper plate on the hill far behind the house. I can still remember the dull thud and puff of gray smoke as it drifted across the terraces.

Dali's action painting such as the use of a sea urchin with ink on its moving spines along with bulletism, ink spilling and splashing with a spatula, etc., were never ends in themselves. The artist would use such props and stunts only as a starter. Then he would take the paper into his studio and finish it up by hand. He did so, so expertly that one could not discern where his work began and where the underlying "accident" left off.

The sea urchin figures large in Dali's life. In his jewel era, he created one with moving spines. The sea urchin shell is featured both in his study for the *Madonna of Port Lligat* which he showed to the Pope in 1948-49 and in the huge final version.

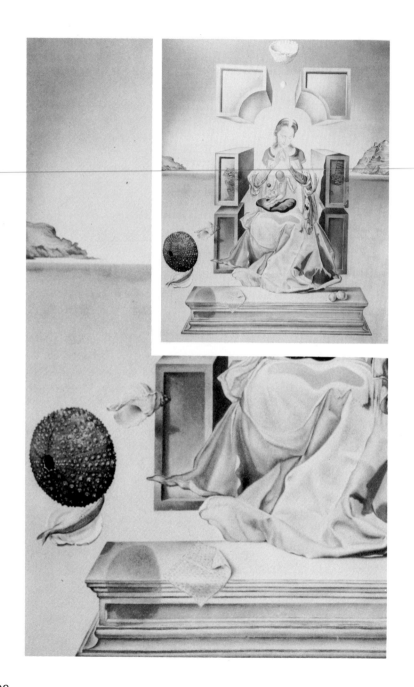

The sea urchin shell is seen again in the foreground of his masterwork *The Discovery of America by Christopher Columbus*. He added the shell of the urchin over my objections that the work was already too cluttered. At the time, the artist had taped a large photographic blowup of the urchin shell in the forefront of the canvas, and I dared to suggest he leave it out. He replied that in time we would understand why he had used it. Well over a decade later Eleanor figured out that it represented Armstrong stepping on the moon. She called Dali and told him of her discovery, and he replied that he was surprised it had taken us so many years to detect his prophecy!

It is interesting to record that in his *Secret Life* in the fifth edition of 1976 on page 409 he describes the title of his *Columbus* as "The Cosmic Dream of Christopher Columbus."

From the swimming we have done around Cape Creus one does not see many sea urchins with the long threatening spines of the West Indies. The ones with short bristles which are edible are much more in evidence and do not appear as menacing as those found in the Caribbean. Suffice it to say, I have seen Dali eat the raw meat of the latter type both on the spot and in his own dining room.

Another example of the sea urchin's shell is seen in *Rhinocerotic Figure of Phidias' Illisos,* discussed under Starfish Q.V.

EXCERPT FROM DALI'S PRIVATE DICTIONARY

The sea urchin, based on the dodecahedron, is a perfect animal. It is the image of heaven.

The Discovery of America by Christopher Columbus — *1958-59*

SERPENTS

(See SNAKES)

SHEEP

The ladies joined us, and in a moment Dali jumped up in great excitement, saying "Sheeps! Sheeps! Look les sheeps!" We all looked for sheep but simply could not see any. On the skyline, however, was the fantastic semi-industrial skyline of Oakland. Again Dali exclaimed "Sheeps! Sheeps!" and it finally dawned on us that he was saying "Ships," for there along the far waterfront were hundreds of boats at anchor, a moth-ball fleet that made an incredible array of naval power against the gray scudding clouds. "Ships" we said. "Yes," Dali replied. "Sheeps! Dali always see everyzing feerst!"

In the 1960's in Paris, we recall going with Dali to the vernissage of a print made from a watercolor by Dali. It was an evening event, and Dali had commanded live sheep. The client did arrange to get several and managed to confine the poor animals to a small portion of the store where they could be seen from the street. Dali's customer

was terrified both of the sheep and the artist, and we left the vernissage accompanying Dali in the Cadillac with mixed emotions of the "event" or happening. We felt the stunt was in bad taste, but the sadistic artist loved it, especially since it had cost his client a bundle of money. When I commented on this to the artist, he popped his brown eyes and said, "much suffering is le best. Myself is like-ee que le client soofer. Le more soofering is better."

SHELLS

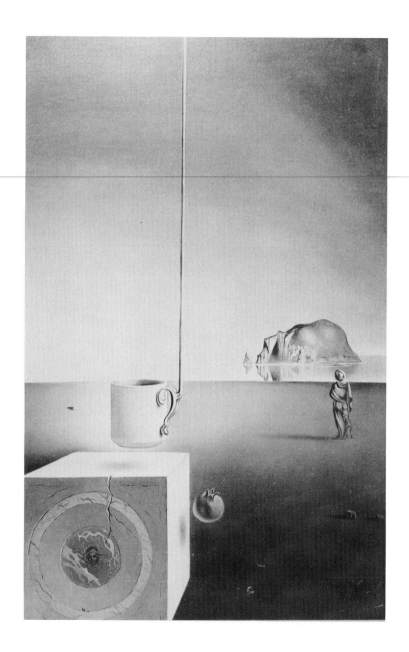

On one occasion I brought Dali an abalone shell as a sort of penance. He at once seized the opportunity to chastise me again for a decision I had made in the mid 1940's not to purchase a small oil titled *Giant Flying Demi-Tasse with Incomprehensible Appendage Five Meters Long*. In Romero's book, *All Dali in One Painting*, the picture is misdated as being of 1932-1935 vintage.

The 1945 work was actually a new version of *True Picture Court of the Isle of the Dead* of 1932. As an excuse for not going out on a limb to purchase the second version of this work, I said that I did not like the color of the square in the lower left. Dali did not let that pass either unnoticed or unforgotten.

Thus some two decades later when I brought him the abalone shell he at once took his revenge. "Morse why is dees, you bring me one shell avec le exact color of le tea cup que you is no buy, et que you is tell you no like-ee le color. Le color is exactly le same of dees shell!" That was a tough one to field, and I am sure my excuse was not the real one, even then. It was that in the mid 1940's and as young marrieds there was a limit to our resources, a good deal of which were tied up in works by Magritte, Miro, Tanguy and de Chirico. Later we sold our surrealist collection and bought more Dali's, but in 1945 we were still, to some degree, hedging our bets on the controversial master as our Dalinian education proceeded. Our art lessons from Dali were always poignant and memorable. Our problem was, however, to remain always out of the spotlight which we felt from that day in April 1943 when we first met the painter, should always be on Dali in center stage—and on him alone.

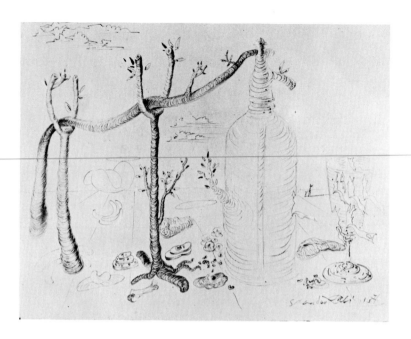

SHRIMP

"**A**h le shrimp. Is one si-fon (syphon). You no know dees? Is appear in le Julien Levy Gallery and make one manifestation pour proof avec le syphon. Myself is create one painting of one syphon (the carbonated gas variety). Le syphon is 'aving one han-dell plus que one meter long. Gala is want make le attachment, mais myself tell que no. Is make one real 'an-dell (handle). Is now possible create avec one man in Paris que make les objects, le shoe, le bread on le head, etc. Is no one gimmick. Is create le seaphone par-ce-que one day is coming le atom bomb et is destruct eversing. Et apres, si is fund (found) le syphon avec le handle one meter long is tell somesing about les peoples que is living before. Is one complete mystification! Ah! le shrimp. Le connection is dees. You no know dees? You is take-ee le moustache de one shrimp, et place in le glass of vater so (illustrating on his Vichy water glass) et le whisker of le shrimp is syphon out le vater. Is possible empty le sea avec one shrimp!"

"Et one time Dali is foods le shrimp (eat). Af-ter is take-ee out le flesh, et foods le flesh, mais is alzo place one leetle piece in one glass of vater. Is take-ee one stick et putsch so. (Here he took a cocktail stirrer, and poked it down in his glass to illustrate how he proded the piece of shrimp meat.) Et le shrimp is que already dead et que y yam eat, is react so. (Here he gestured to show how the corpse of the shrimp rejected the probing of his stick.) Is proof que le shrimp is moving, even si le shrimp is already in stomach of Dali!"

Shortly before we got to Del Monte Lodge, Dali came to life as he spotted known landmarks. He began telling us about his catching fresh-water shrimp in the Carmel River. He insisted we should get a boat and go shrimping, and he could not understand why the Americans did not catch and eat them, because to him they were a great delicacy.

He was, of course, refering to what we call crawfish and which is not widely eaten in America, and probably with good reason. I recall one day when Eleanor and I were driving from Paris to Port Lligat, somewhere below Paris we stopped at a local Inn and Eleanor had what we called "shrimp" but which in fact were crawfish from local streams. She was made extremely ill from the animals and spent a miserable two days recovering en route.

When we first visited Spain in 1954 we were quite taken with the fact that most of the fishermen's boats had clusters of lamps in the bow. They were used for night fishing and shrimping. Today these large picturesque bowl like lamps are not nearly so plentiful as they used to be.

Increasingly the Gulf of Lyons and the northern coastal waters are being relentlessly fished out. And all sorts of sea food are becoming increasingly scarce and more expensive. Indeed the skin divers are taking just about everything including sea urchins. The lovely bays of Cape Creus we remember as havens for fish and langousta are becoming more sterile and lifeless each year. The French who come to the area in hordes with their rubber boats, are being driven southward into Spanish waters leaving a growing sub-marine desolation where once all sorts of sea animals proliferated. Shrimp per se were more a feature of Dali's diet than of his art, while even the net menders of yesterday are less and less visible, as the sea becomes always more nearly fished out.

Our own observations swimming and snorkeling off Cape Creus confirm this strange underwater desolation. In Port Lligat we have repeatedly been appalled to see the hordes of French and Spanish swimmers unloading their boats and fishing equipment. In past years it was Dali's magic presence that drew the throngs over the coastal mountains to Port Lligat. Today it is the skin divers who flock there with nary a glance at the painter's now somewhat delapidated residence expanded from a fisherman's barracks of the 1920's. Such "progress" will soon destroy the pristine beauty of Dali's beloved mountain rimmed bay if the authorities do not curb both tourism and urbanization of this unique and historic locale, along with skin diving fishermen who are now stripping the sea bottoms bare.

SNAILS

The artist relished snails and we often started our meals together with escargot. In 1989 on a trip into Cathare county just north of the Spanish border with Meli and Pascual, the photographer had us all gathering French snails for domesticating in the garden beside his house in Figueres.

Dali's nipples becoming snails may be a little upsetting, interesting though the exercise is. The spiral aspect of the snail's shell, however is quite another matter. Its esthetic roots, of course, date back to the Parthenon and the golden section from which the galactic spiral is mathematically derived. We can all be grateful to Matila Ghyka, the French esthethetician whom Dali met in the 1940's in Carmel. This introduced a whole new dimension of classical mise en pages into Dali's works which both stabilized their structure and involved a strict mathematical discipline, of which few artists today are even aware. The snail and its spiral thus bear a definite relationship to his art of which all too few viewers are ever even remotely aware.

216

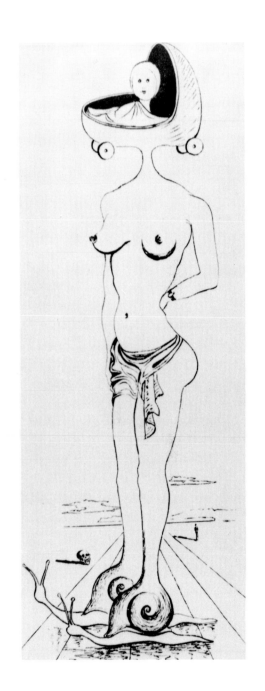

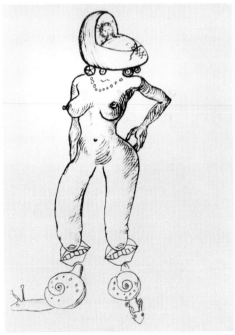

That the study of the basic structure of many of Dali's works stems from the spiral derived from the Golden Rectangle has been totally overlooked both by his critics and his biographers. To me it was a formidable adventure and an unending challenge. Thus it was Dali who taught me that our spiral galaxy is repeated in the shell of a snail. There are no harmonies in a taper, while the whole universe relates to "le as-peer-all" as Dali called the spiral, and today I use it in several of my company's products with extraordinary results, thanks to Dali!

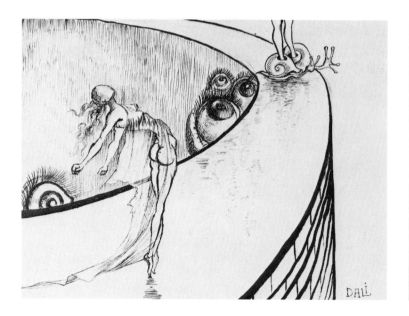

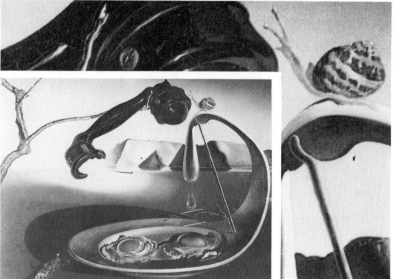

SNAKES

In all my conversations with Dali from day one (April 1943) in the St. Regis Hotel to my last sight of him in Puiguert Clinic in Barcelona in 1981. I do not recall the subject of snakes ever appearing in his bestiary.

The first appearance of snakes was, I believe, in the 1940 oil titled historically *Visage of War*. It was a sticky painting which as young collectors we could not bring ourselves to buy. I felt it was prophetic, but Eleanor did not care for the serpents and the gruesomeness of the war theme as we were living from month to month under the shadow of the draft. (As I was involved with machine tools, an essential industry, I was not called up.) The Dalis were, of course, in exile in America; and while we kept up with them by phone and letters, we did not see them as frequently as after the war ended and we could get to New York more often. *Visage of War* frequently came up, but we never could bring ourselves to buy it, prophetic though it was.

In fairness to the painting, it evolved just when the Dalis were between agents. Their loyal supporter Julien Levy was phasing out of the business, and while Dali just had made a connection with Knoedler's, it was rather odd because the staid old gallery mainly represented the world of old masters. And Georges Keller's less known Bignou Gallery (later Carstairs) was where most of his 1940's works were shown.

During the 1940's Dali did many remarkable illustrated editions and serpents are found here and there, but they were never really featured in either his oeuvre or conversations.

Visage of War – *1940*

219

In all our wanderings and mountain climbs in Ampurdan, we have never seen a snake in our thirty six years of explorations.

A typical example of Dali's work as an illustrator is found on page 25 of Maurice Sandoz' *The House Without Windows* (1950). There the artist drew three serpents whose writhings repeat themselves in the form of adjacent tree roots. It was inspired by the mention in the text on page 25 where a piano tuner was left in the music room believing a boa constrictor on a pedestal was stuffed. When he finished his work the "stuffed" boa was gone! The Dali-Sandoz team also produced another volume titled *On The Verge* (1950) where the frontispiece showed two butterflies and a shrunken head. So far, Dali has not yet been recognized as one of the great illustrators of the 20th Century.

SPHINX

(Also See BAT)

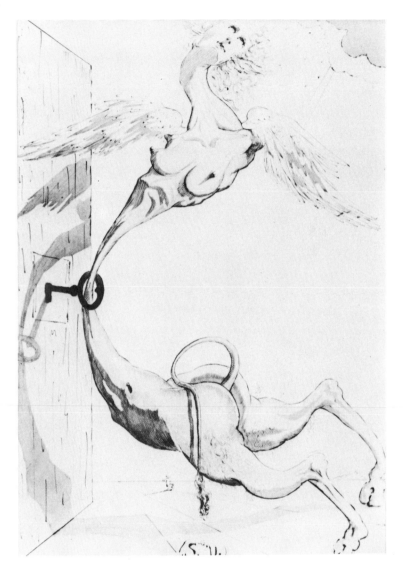

While Dali's sphinx of *Shirley Temple* is a strong whimsey aimed at destroying the then popular hero worship being accorded the youthful actress, Dali's versions of the monster received many treatments. Typical of his inventiveness to add freshness to his bestiary was *Sphinx Passing Through the Eye of a Key* of 1953, a disturbing sepia ink and watercolor work which strains the limitations of the word: "Any Egyptian statue or figure having typically, the body of a lion, and the head of a man, ram or hawk." Paramount of course, is the image of the Egyptian Sphinx at Giza.

Sphinx Passing Through the Eye of a Key — *1953*

221

The Greek concept is that of "a winged monster with a lion's body and the head and breasts of a woman, specifically a monster of this kind that perched on a rock near Thebes and asked a riddle of every passerby, strangling all who could not answer. Oedipus solved the riddle, and the Sphinx killed herself (himself?)."

This sort of occasional Dali works, especially in watercolor, have not been either cataloged or really integrated in Dali's oeuvre, and as a result many of his works on paper remain virtually unknown. There has never been a show of his watercolors. It is an area that involves animals of many sorts, though I think that flowers and angels would predominate were it possible to get together a book on Dali's superb watercolors over the years. Many were sold directly to friends and clients.

Eleanor and I toyed with Dali's *Shirley Temple* for some two decades and could never bring ourselves to pay the asked price—well over $25,000 as I recall it.

"Shirley Temple, Le plus jeune monstre sacré du cinema de son temps," — *1939*

222

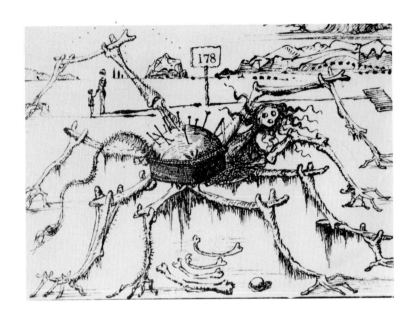

SPIDERS

Dali's use of spiders was mainly in various illustrations. They were usually depicted as being very large. Considering how closely Dali observed insects, it is interesting that the artist rarely drew a spider actual size as he did so frequently with ants. The unique spider seen in Chant 17 of Dali's version of Dante's *Divine Comedy* is quite typical of the artist's approach to this bug, embellished as it is with a familiar torso and head. Dali's inventiveness and the freshness of his illustrations remain a rather neglected facet of his overall genius.

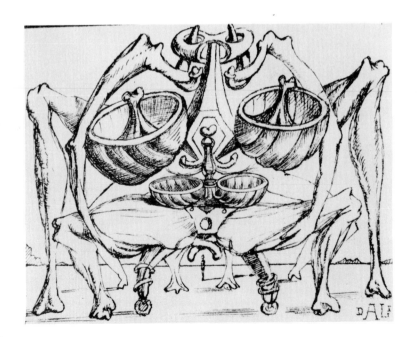

223

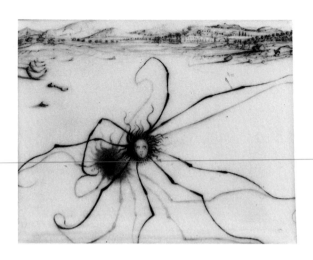
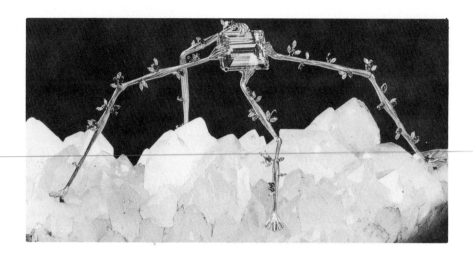

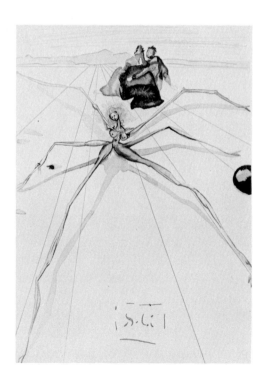

STARFISH

Much of Dali's bestiary consists of relatively small details which casual viewers often tend to miss. A fine example of this sort of invisibility is the starfish in the lower left of Dali's large work called *Rhinocerotic Figure of Phidias' Illisos* of 1954. (Here is also seen the dried shell of a sea urchin Q.V. Note the appearance of the rhinoceros horn discussed under that heading.)

The Catalan artist also made a series of very unusual ceramic tiles, each with an individual design. These are 7½" square and appeared not only in the original edition, but also in a second one. The starfish which is seen on one of these tiles is probably the most striking of the set of six pieces. It is also possible that in the early thirties, Dali used the starfish in a design for Madame Chanel.

SWALLOWS

The unveiling in Barcelona in 1969 of Dali's ceiling three meters in diameter in the Palacete Albéniz on Montjuich and titled *Horadela Monarquia* sticks in my mind because it was dedicated at the very beginning of the subsequent vast Dali frauds. It was especially memorable because it was also the day I had it out with both Moore and Dali, but separately, on the matter of his signed works on paper that were already being misrepresented as "original lithographs" at point of sale. These, were wrongly touted as sure to be "good investments," and "bound to increase in value." This was unlikely because the editions were virtually unlimited, and were merely reproductions and quite high priced. The confrontations began when I mentioned the reproductions to Dali in Barcelona as we were en route to see the new painting now mounted in the ceiling of the "Little Palace" where the king stays when visiting Barcelona.

The canvas shows a circle of Sardanas dancers seen from underneath. There are some eighteen identifiable swallows arranged in a spiral that appear to be flying off into the sky. The impressive work is titled *Hour of the Monarchy* or on occasion, *The Royal Hour*.

We were in two taxis and at a traffic light when Dali made me get out of his cab and get into Moore's. There I faced the dapper fellow, on the long term impact of his plans to wholesale Dali's images in reproduction and present them as lithographs by Dali. To misrepresent them as lithographs or originals of any sort, I said, could have enormous repercussions down the line. He was fully aware of Dali's greed and his own and that they were only mechanical reproductions of Dali's watercolors and oils. Being on the road to his own exit, Moore was not about to heed any warning of future complications arriving from reproductions of Dalinian images and art works as "signed" editions. He wanted money now and the future be damned.

Moore's position was that Dali's original works were now increasingly rare and expensive. If reproductions of his paintings were mass-produced and duly signed by the artist, they would give others than ourselves a chance to house and enjoy Dali's famous images. It all sounded innocuous enough, with both the artist and his aide being interested only in one thing: easy money.

It was a tense session indeed involving the greed both of Dali and Moore. My temerity in meddling in it at all and foretelling future frauds thus fell on two sets of deaf ears, for a conjoint avarice was clearly at the root of this scenario for proliferation of Dali works on paper using printing presses and a penciled signature to create an "original" of any sort. At the time some fifteen years ago, I felt we stood on the brink of a Niagara. Today—in 1992—I am astounded at the brashness I exhibited as I evaluated Moore's attempts to make as much money as fast as he could out of Dali before Sabater was fully installed as Dali's new manager, secretary or aide. Neither man was paid by Dali, as we begged Dali to do, thus the fellows had to live by their wits—and this they did very well. The artist should have held a much tighter reign on his aides and kept a more business-like grip on their activities by making them fully accountable for the fraudulent misrepresentations that would be made at point of sale.

227

And the doughty fierce Gala? As long ago as 1965 she had countenanced the integration of Moore into the menage. She was clearly getting tired and bored with being Dali's salesperson and only factotum. This included all the various logistics involved in his travels, the care and pricing of the paintings and being Queen of Dali's motley court as well, for months of December to May when they habitually traveled to Paris, New York, Madrid, and Barcelona.

It was just at this heated moment that we went to Port Lligat with the Dalis, as it bridged the logistical gap between the end of Moore's reign and the start of Sabater's as Dali's general factotum promoter — and as it proved — exploiter. This was because, of course, they had to live by their ability to deal both with Dali and the purchasers of the given contracts of which there many. These deals were usually bonafide up until 1978 when Center Art Gallery got into the act, and Marchand, Hamon, Delcourt, and other real art gangsters, came along. Then the printing presses really started rolling, and the Dali signature forgers swung into action, and the rip-offs began which culminated in the Center Art Gallery trial in Honolulu.

Thus when one mentions swallows to me, the birds in *Hour of the Monarchy* trigger the still disturbing memory of the moment when I was naive enough to stand at the edge of Dali's perilous ocean and try to command the tide not to come in!

And speaking of birds in general, Dali always used a stuffed bird, whether a swallow or swan. When Emily Genauer, the dominant art critic in New York during the 1940's and 1950's, said that the swallow in *Nature Morte Vivante* looked "artificial," I showed the notice to Dali.

He handed it back and said, "Myself is painting precisely que y am see. Is one bird stuff-ed que is exist in le studio. Is not possible putsch one life bird in le house pour paint. Myself is theenk dees voman's is no expected one model. Mais in any way is no important."

In Dali's library in Port Lligat are found two stuffed swans atop the bookcases over the fireplace. Jordi Casals photographed Eleanor and myself in the library in May 1992. I recall that the critic Emily Genauer once critized Dali's depiction of a swan saying it was unlifelike. When Dali read the article he said "Dees vomans is no know nossing. Myself is like-ee very much les stuffed animals, and is painting precisely que y am seeing!"

SWANS

"In le case of les swans, myself is possess-ed ten, perhaps seven, mais in any way, many." "Aren't they dangerous?" Eleanor asked. "No, not avec Gala et moi. Is make one crown, le crown of lights, pour putsch in le head of the swan!"

It was rather early on, say around 1956, that Dali's swans appeared incongruously in Port Lligat. They quickly dominated the sea gulls. For a decade or so the birds floated regally in the blue bay. On one occasion I recall they disappeared and were found somewhere around Cape Norfeu. When one of the birds was killed, as Dali describes in the following excerpt from *Diary of a Genius,* we had some debate over what should be done about getting some company for the remaining one. Gala did locate one and again the birds floated around in the Bay of Port Lligat. I never felt they took to sea water very well and eventually they simply disappeared and the Dalis never replaced them.

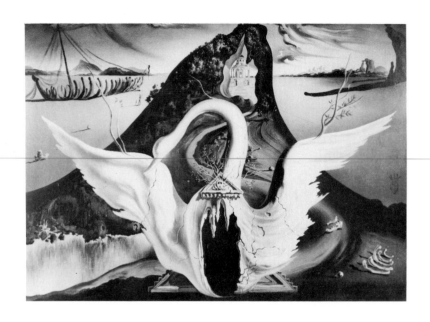

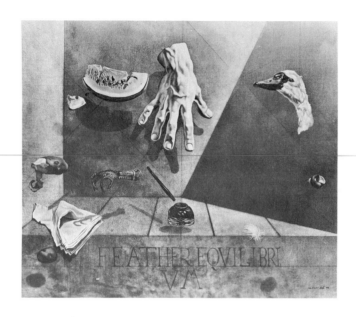

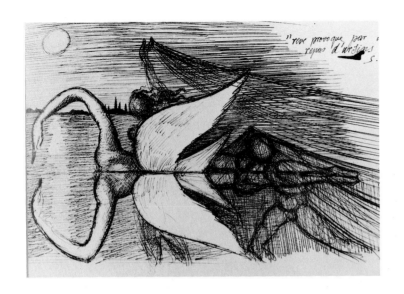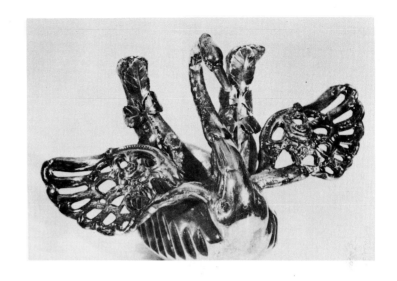

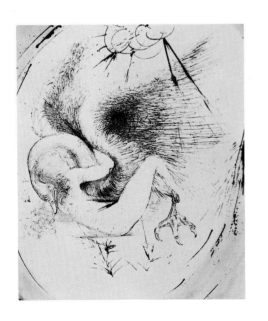

Diary of a Genius

Page 39, July 9th, 1952
Prentice Hall, 1986 ed.

Deliciously aching with the desire to outdo myself. This divine dissatisfaction is the sign that something is growing inside my soul that will give me great satisfaction. At dusk I look out the window at Gala, who seems to me to look even younger than the evening before. She is sailing in her new boat. In passing, she tries to caress our two swans that are standing on a little dinghy. But one flies off and the other hides under the bow.

September 7th, 1956

Today is Sunday. I woke up very late. When I looked out of the window I saw stepping out of a boat one of the Negroes who are camping in the neighborhood. He is covered with blood and carries in his arms one of our swans that is wounded and dying. A tourist has harpooned it, thinking he had discovered a rare bird. This sight affords me a strangely pleasant sadness. Gala comes running out of the house to embrace the swan. At that moment a noise is heard that makes us all jump. With a great deal of noise, a truckload of anthracite for the furnace is being dumped. That truck is the catalytic agent of the myth. In our day one can divine the actions of Jupiter, if one is watchful, in the unexpected presence of trucks that are big enough so that you cannot help seeing them.

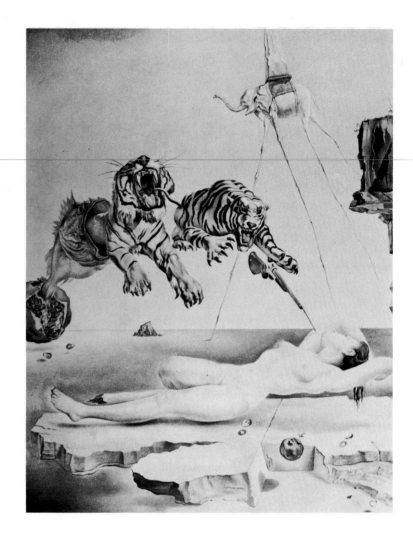

TIGERS

Dali's use of tigers was limited primarily to two of his paintings, both of which we considered but did not buy. The first was a nude, ostensibly Gala, awakening from a dream. A spindle legged elephant is in the background and two Barnum and Bailey tigers are leaping through the air, with the left one emerging from the mouth of a fish. This work is now in the Baron Von Thyssen Collection destined for Spain.

The other tiger was done in 1963. It is a sort of puzzle as it conceals the image of a tiger emerging from a field of squares, as well as three Lenins masquerading as Chinamen. We felt it was far too contrived, and of course it was totally overshaded by *The Battle of Tetuan* (see Horse).

This brings up the question of Dali's unsold canvases. Typically he reserved the very best piece in every show "for Gala," saying it was reserved for her as a gift. The balance of the works left unsold went into storage and became part of Dali's own collection. The 1963 tiger is a good example of a Dali that was exhibited at one of his biannual shows and which never found a buyer for a long time thereafter.

It should be noted that the Dalis feared being poor above anything else. Their horded canvases, which he told us many times were destined for his museum in Figueres, were their hedge against the contingencies of old age. Thus like all Catalonians we were dreadfully shocked that a later and questionable will left all his collection to Madrid, including his 1963 tiger. It is interesting that despite Dali's ploy of seeming to give Gala certain works, he never formally did so. Thus at Gala's death she had no legal title to any of the art collection at all! Today waves of suspicion still arise about the mechanics involved in changing Dali's will when he was well known to be almost totally incapacitated. A full accounting is long overdue Dali's public to remove the many doubts about his will, and what happened to the painter's considerable fortune during his sad decade of incompetence.

Fifty abstract pictures which as seen from two yards change into three Lenins masquerading as Chinese, and as seen from six yards appear as the head of a royal tiger — *1963*

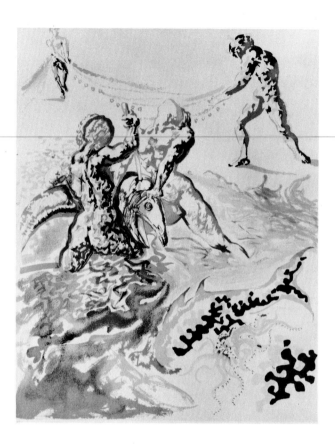

TUNA

Dali got onto stuffed animals again and said, "No forget que y yam possess-ed of one stuffed tuna que somebody is gift me for use in *Tuna Fishing.*"

The painter's major canvas *Tuna Fishing* was a reflection of both POP and OP art, though Dali never paid much attention to either of these two brief contemporary movements. Pop Art he said he invented in the 30's with his *Venus with Drawers,* etc., and he would not go back to it. OP art was mainly Vassarely's field and Dali went directly away from such orderly ordinary optical figures to the most disorderly possible. Thus much of the painting in *Tuna Fishing* is done in a squiggly style which is both colorful and not boring either in form or palette.

This picture, a large one, was stolen from the owner's island home on the Riviera. It was later recovered rolled and discarded. No reason for the theft was ever given unless it was done just to prove no man's castle is impenetrable. Ricard, the owner is a maker of a popular French liqueur (Absinthe) and bought the painting directly from Dali. The artist's descriptions of watching the tuna fishing off the rocky coast just south of Rosas were gory indeed, and the youthful memories they left are reflected in the complex activities going on in this challenging canvas. He told me he often went there with his father, and that the tuna run was a bloody business, but a critical one to the region and its economy.

Tuna Fishing of 1966-67 came as near abstract expressionism (or impressionism) as Dali ever got. It stood in stunning contrast when it was shown in Rotterdam, with the many newly discovered works of the 1930's from the Edward F.W. James Collection. It was fascinating to hear Dali tell how he derived the triangular format from Gericault's famous *Raft of Medusa* in the Louvre.

Tuna Fishing — *1966-67*

TURKEY

Each "hunting season" Dali always had a favorite theme story. He would relate it over and over to his ever changing audience of admirers. One year his stock theme was how to cook a turkey alive and without killing it in the process.

First, he said, one had to catch the turkey, and pull out its feathers. Then you build a fire in the fireplace, not too big and not too small. Then you place the turkey in front of it. Soon the turkey would start to perspire and you took a towel, wiped off all perspiration, especially from its head and around its eyes.

Then when it perspired again, you wiped it off again with a fresh cool towel. If one kept this up long enough, he said, you could eventually cook the bird without killing it.

What made the narration—and the story—so funny, of course, was Dali's telling of it, as he would demonstrate how to wipe the turkey's head by using his handkerchief on his own face. He was a supreme actor and the empathy with the victims as he demonstrated the roasting, kept his guests in gales of laughter.

What topped off the live turkey roast, however, came about when Eleanor asked Gala what he really knew about cooking a turkey. Gala (not much amused by the often repeated story) told Eleanor "the man doesn't know a thing about cooking a turkey. In fact he has never even tasted turkey meat!"

This is the spot to note again that Dali's annual theme narration was repeated over and over to each new audience. Thus once one heard the master's current dissertation each season, one could be fairly sure of not missing anything as he moved from Paris to New York, Madrid and Barcelona and back to Port Lligat for the spring, summer and fall.

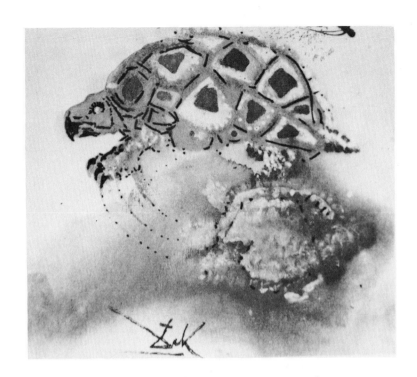

TURTLE

"Myself is trap one turtle. One living turtle. Et is fasten one candle to le back of le turtle, et is move around le table pour illumine le room. Et also is take-ee one ash tray que y yam make. Is kill one turtle, et is make le ash tray from le shell of le turtle que is dead. Is turn le shell upside down et fasten to le back of le udder turtle et putsch on le table. Le turtle is move about le table pour catch les ashes. Is le first living ash-tray."

In one of the many privately printed Dali books I published over the years, I ran a picture of the artist from the files. When I gave him a copy of the book, he looked at the photo of himself and said "Morse, why is you exhibit dees picture of Dali? Myself is look like one old turtle. Is necessary you choice one udder." (The word in Dali's language came out as tour-tell).

239

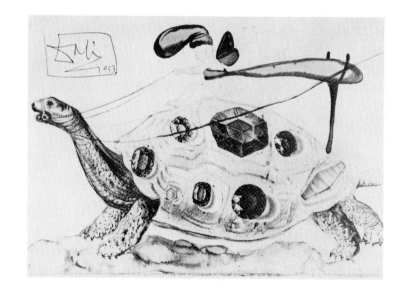

240

UNICORNS

Without a total search of every Dali illustration, it would be impossible to locate all his references to unicorns and all other imaginary beasts. One is seen in his study for the ballet *"Des Vendangeurs."*

WORMS

As a young man (boy) Dali often visited the Muli de la Torre, the Pitchot's farm near Figueres. There he at one time painted a series of cherries, using a door. It was truly a remarkable achievement and totally realistic—so much so someone tried to pick a cherry out of it.

In one of the cherries he used as a model, he said he found a worm. He used a pin to pick the worm out of the cherry—an experience he never forgot, as he said one might easily have eaten it.

Several searches were made of Muli de la Torre, a remarkably preserved working farm of the late 1800's with water generated power, for the painted door of Dali's youth but it was never found.

A worm is seen in one of the artist's illustrations for his *Alice in Wonderland*.

EXCERPT FROM DALI'S PRIVATE DICTIONARY

DISMAL OR IMMORTAL WORMS (in Picasso)

They have this name because of their disagreeable aspect; all are cross-eyed... Immortal because no matter how many times one cuts their head, it reproduces in an amazing manner.

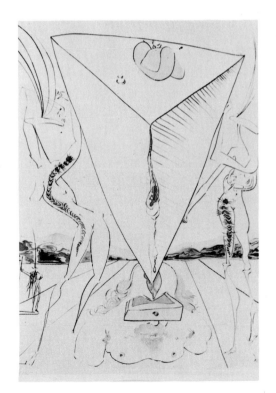